SOFTWARE
FOR
DEPENDABLE
SYSTEMS

SUFFICIENT EVIDENCE?

Daniel Jackson, Martyn Thomas, and Lynette I. Millett, Editors

Committee on Certifiably Dependable Software Systems

Computer Science and Telecommunications Board

Division on Engineering and Physical Sciences

NATIONAL RESEARCH COUNCIL
OF THE NATIONAL ACADEMIES

THE NATIONAL ACADEMIES PRESS
Washington, D.C.
www.nap.edu

THE NATIONAL ACADEMIES PRESS   500 Fifth Street, N.W.   Washington, DC 20001

NOTICE: The project that is the subject of this report was approved by the Governing Board of the National Research Council, whose members are drawn from the councils of the National Academy of Sciences, the National Academy of Engineering, and the Institute of Medicine. The members of the committee responsible for the report were chosen for their special competences and with regard for appropriate balance.

Support for this project was provided by the National Science Foundation and the National Security Agency under sponsor award number CCR-0236725; the Office of Naval Research under sponsor award number N00014-03-1-0915; and the National Science Foundation, the National Security Agency, and the Federal Aviation Administration under sponsor award number CNS-0342801. Any opinions, findings, or recommendations expressed in this publication are those of the authors and do not necessarily reflect the views of the agencies and organizations that provided support for the project.

International Standard Book Number-13: 978-0-309-10394-7
International Standard Book Number-10: 0-309-10394-0

Additional copies of this report are available from

The National Academies Press
500 Fifth Street, N.W., Lockbox 285
Washington, DC 20055
(800) 624-6242
(202) 334-3313 (in the Washington metropolitan area)
http://www.nap.edu

Printed in the United States of America

THE NATIONAL ACADEMIES
Advisers to the Nation on Science, Engineering, and Medicine

The **National Academy of Sciences** is a private, nonprofit, self-perpetuating society of distinguished scholars engaged in scientific and engineering research, dedicated to the furtherance of science and technology and to their use for the general welfare. Upon the authority of the charter granted to it by the Congress in 1863, the Academy has a mandate that requires it to advise the federal government on scientific and technical matters. Dr. Ralph J. Cicerone is president of the National Academy of Sciences.

The **National Academy of Engineering** was established in 1964, under the charter of the National Academy of Sciences, as a parallel organization of outstanding engineers. It is autonomous in its administration and in the selection of its members, sharing with the National Academy of Sciences the responsibility for advising the federal government. The National Academy of Engineering also sponsors engineering programs aimed at meeting national needs, encourages education and research, and recognizes the superior achievements of engineers. Dr. Charles M. Vest is president of the National Academy of Engineering.

The **Institute of Medicine** was established in 1970 by the National Academy of Sciences to secure the services of eminent members of appropriate professions in the examination of policy matters pertaining to the health of the public. The Institute acts under the responsibility given to the National Academy of Sciences by its congressional charter to be an adviser to the federal government and, upon its own initiative, to identify issues of medical care, research, and education. Dr. Harvey V. Fineberg is president of the Institute of Medicine.

The **National Research Council** was organized by the National Academy of Sciences in 1916 to associate the broad community of science and technology with the Academy's purposes of furthering knowledge and advising the federal government. Functioning in accordance with general policies determined by the Academy, the Council has become the principal operating agency of both the National Academy of Sciences and the National Academy of Engineering in providing services to the government, the public, and the scientific and engineering communities. The Council is administered jointly by both Academies and the Institute of Medicine. Dr. Ralph J. Cicerone and Dr. Charles M. Vest are chair and vice chair, respectively, of the National Research Council.

www.national-academies.org

Preface

Critical systems are often subject to certification: a formal assurance that the system has met relevant technical standards designed to ensure it will not unduly endanger the public and can be depended upon to deliver its intended service safely and securely. Today, certification[1] of the dependability of a software-based system usually relies more on assessments of the process used to develop the system than on the properties of the system itself. While these assessments can be useful, few would dispute that direct observation of the artifact ought to provide a stronger kind of assurance than the credentials of its production method. Yet the complexity of software systems, as well as the discontinuous way they behave, renders them extremely difficult to analyze unless great care has been taken with their structure and maintenance.

To further understand these and related issues, the High Confidence Software and Systems (HCSS) Coordinating Group (CG) of the National Science and Technology Council's Networking and Information Technology Research and Development (NITRD) Subcommittee initiated discussions with the Computer Science and Telecommunications Board (CSTB) of the National Research Council (NRC). These discussions resulted in a study to assess the current state of certification in dependable systems with the goal of recommending areas for improvement. Funding

---

[1]The committee uses the term "certification" to refer to the process of assuring that a product or process has certain stated properties, which are then recorded in a certificate. Certification usually involves assurance by an independent party, although the term is also used analogously for customer (second-party) and developer (first-party) assurance.

for the project was obtained from the following HCSS CG agencies: the National Science Foundation, the National Security Agency, the Office of Naval Research, and the Federal Aviation Administration.

A committee was formed consisting of 13 experts from industry and academia specializing in diverse aspects of systems dependability including software engineering, software testing and evaluation, software dependability, embedded systems, human-computer interaction, systems engineering, systems architecture, accident theory, standards setting, avionics, medicine, economics, security, and regulatory policy (see Appendix A for committee and staff biographies).

To accomplish its mission, the committee divided the study into two phases: a framing phase and an assessment phase. The framing phase culminated in a public workshop in April 2004, attended by members of industry, government, and academia. The workshop was organized as a series of panel discussions on a variety of topics and was summarized by the committee in a subsequent report.[2]

In the assessment phase of the study, the committee held a series of meetings over a 2-year period. Each meeting comprised a day of open sessions in which the committee heard opinions and evidence from a variety of experts, and 1 or 2 days of closed sessions in which the committee analyzed the information presented to it and worked to develop a view on the state of software dependability and recommendations for the future. The chair of the committee also conducted a handful of telephone interviews with experts to supplement the material covered during the committee's meetings.

This report adopts a broad perspective on the question of how software might be made dependable in a cost-effective manner rather than focusing narrowly on the question of software certification per se. By design, this diverse committee represented a range of views on issues, and with this wider perspective, the committee found itself confronting the perennial dilemmas of software engineering, discussing in a current context many of the same issues that have been debated since a seminal 1968 NATO conference.[3] In discussions and through the process of writing the report, a number of these issues were explored, including the likelihood of catastrophes caused by software; whether formal methods will scale to large systems; and the extent to which a manufacturer's disclaim-

[2]National Research Council, 2004, *Summary of a Workshop on Software Certification and Dependability*, The National Academies Press, Washington, D.C. Available online at <http://books.nap.edu/catalog/11133.html>.

[3]See P. Naur and B. Randell, eds., 1969, "Software engineering: Report on a conference sponsored by the NATO Science Committee," Garmisch, Germany, October 7-11, 1968, NATO Scientific Affairs Division, Brussels, Belgium. Available online at <http://homepages.cs.ncl.ac.uk/brian.randell/NATO/>.

ing of liability should be seen as undermining any dependability claims it makes. Although this study does not attempt to resolve these long-standing issues, the committee believes that the recommendations and approach set forth in this report can be used in the short term to improve the dependability of systems and in the longer term to lay the foundation for new and more powerful software development methods.

The committee thanks the many individuals who contributed to its work. The people who briefed the committee at the workshop and in subsequent meetings are listed in Appendix B; we appreciated their willingness to address the questions we posed to them and are grateful for their insights. The sponsors of the report have been most supportive and responsive in helping the committee to do its work. The reviewers and the review monitor, listed below, provided thoughtful and detailed critiques that influenced the final form of the report significantly.

My personal thanks to Martyn Thomas, who from the start took a leading role in helping to crystallize the committee's thinking and shared much of the burden of writing and editing the report; to Lynette Millett, our study director, for her constructive guidance throughout, for keeping us focused, and for her expert editing of the report; to associate program officer David Padgham for his meticulous help with the preparation of the final version; to our research associate at the start of the study, Phil Hilliard, for gathering materials and setting up our infrastructure; to my doctoral student, Derek Wayside, for configuring and maintaining the committee Wiki; to Liz Fikre of the DEPS editorial staff for her careful and clarifying assistance with manuscript preparation; to review monitor Elsa Garmire for her thorough and helpful oversight; and to Jon Eisenberg, director of the CSTB, for the special interest he has taken in this study and the attention and sage advice he has given.

Daniel Jackson, *Chair*
Committee on Certifiably
Dependable Software Systems

Acknowledgment of Reviewers

This report has been reviewed in draft form by individuals chosen for their diverse perspectives and technical expertise, in accordance with procedures approved by the National Research Council's (NRC's) Report Review Committee. The purpose of this independent review is to provide candid and critical comments that will assist the institution in making its published report as sound as possible and to ensure that the report meets institutional standards for objectivity, evidence, and responsiveness to the study charge. The review comments and draft manuscript remain confidential to protect the integrity of the deliberative process. We wish to thank the following individuals for their review of this report:

Ashish Arora, Carnegie Mellon University,
David Corman, Boeing Company,
Steven Fenves, Carnegie Mellon University,
R. John Hansman, Massachusetts Institute of Technology,
Butler Lampson, Microsoft Corporation,
Jesse H. Poore, University of Tennessee,
Tariq Samad, Honeywell Automation and Control Solutions,
Alfred Z. Spector, Independent Consultant, and
William Stead, Vanderbilt University.

Although the reviewers listed above have provided many constructive comments and suggestions, they were not asked to endorse the conclusions or recommendations, nor did they see the final draft of the report before its release. The review of this report was overseen by Elsa Garmire of Dartmouth University. Appointed by the NRC, she was responsible for making certain that an independent examination of this report was carried out in accordance with institutional procedures and that all review comments were carefully considered. Responsibility for the final content of this report rests entirely with the authoring committee and the institution.

Contents

Summary

How can software and the systems that rely on it be made dependable in a cost-effective manner, and how can one obtain assurance that dependability has been achieved? Rather than focusing narrowly on the question of software or system certification per se, this report adopts a broader perspective.

A system is dependable when it can be depended on to produce the consequences for which it was designed, and no adverse effects, in its intended environment. This means, first and foremost, that the term dependability has no useful meaning for a given system until these consequences and the intended environment are made explicit by a clear prioritization of the requirements of the system and an articulation of environmental assumptions. The effects of software are felt in the physical, human, and organizational environment in which it operates, so dependability should be understood in that context and cannot be reduced easily to local properties, such as resilience to crashing or conformance to a protocol. Humans who interact with the software should be viewed not as external and beyond the boundary of the software engineer's concerns but as an integral part of the system. Failures involving human operators should not automatically be assumed to be the result of errors of usage; rather, the role of design flaws should be considered as well as the role of the human operator. As a consequence, a systems engineering approach—which views the software as one engineered artifact in a larger system of many components, some engineered and some given, and the pursuit of dependability as a balancing of costs and benefits and a prioritization of risks—is vital.

Unfortunately, it is difficult to assess the dependability of software. The field of software engineering suffers from a pervasive lack of evidence about the incidence and severity of software failures; about the dependability of existing software systems; about the efficacy of existing and proposed development methods; about the benefits of certification schemes; and so on. There are many anecdotal reports, which—although often useful for indicating areas of concern or highlighting promising avenues of research—do little to establish a sound and complete basis for making policy decisions regarding dependability. Moreover, there is sometimes an implicit assumption that adhering to particular process strictures guarantees certain levels of dependability. The committee regards claims of extraordinary dependability that are sometimes made on this basis for the most critical of systems as unsubstantiated, and perhaps irresponsible. This difficulty regarding the lack of evidence for system dependability leads to two conclusions, reflected in the committee's findings and recommendations below: (1) that better evidence is needed, so that approaches aimed at improving the dependability of software can be objectively assessed, and (2) that, for now, the pursuit of dependability in software systems should focus on the construction and evaluation of evidence.

The committee thus subscribes to the view that software is "guilty until proven innocent," and that the burden of proof falls on the developer to convince the certifier or regulator that the software is dependable. This approach is not novel and is becoming standard in the world of systems safety, in which an explicit safety case (and not merely adherence to good practice) is usually required. Similarly, a software system should be regarded as dependable only if it has a credible dependability case, the elements of which are described below.

Meeting the burden of proof for dependability will be challenging. The demand for credible evidence will, in practice, make it infeasible to develop highly dependable systems in a cost-effective way without some radical changes in priorities. If very high dependability is to be achieved at reasonable cost, the needs of the dependability case will influence many aspects of the development, including the choice of programming language and the software architecture, and simplicity will be key. For high levels of dependability, the evidence provided by testing alone will rarely suffice and will have to be augmented by analysis. The ability to make independence arguments that allow global properties to be inferred from an analysis of a relatively small part of the system will be essential. Rigorous processes will be needed to ensure that the chain of evidence for dependability claims is preserved.

The committee also recognized the importance of adopting the practices that are already known and used by the best developers; this summary gives a sample of such practices in more detail below. Some of these (such as systematic configuration management and automated regression testing) are relatively easy to adopt; others (such as constructing hazard analyses and threat models, exploiting formal notations when appropriate, and applying static analysis to code) will require new training for many developers. However valuable, though, these practices are in themselves no silver bullet, and new techniques and methods will be required in order to build future software systems to the level of dependability that will be required.

ASSESSMENT

Society is increasingly dependent on software. Software failures can cause or contribute to serious accidents that result in death, injury, significant environmental damage, or major financial loss. Such accidents have already occurred, and, without intervention, the increasingly pervasive use of software—especially in arenas such as transportation, health care, and the broader infrastructure—may make them more frequent and more serious. In the future, more pervasive deployment of software in the civic infrastructure could lead to more catastrophic failures unless improvements are made.

Software, according to a popular view, fails because of bugs: errors in the code that cause a program to fail to meet its specification. In fact, only a tiny proportion of failures can be attributed to bugs. As is well known to software engineers, by far the largest class of problems arises from errors made in the eliciting, recording, and analysis of requirements. A second major class of problems arises from poor human factors design. The two classes are related; bad user interfaces usually reflect an inadequate understanding of the user's domain and the absence of a coherent and well-articulated conceptual model. Security vulnerabilities are to some extent an exception to this observation: The overwhelming majority of security vulnerabilities reported in software products—and exploited to attack the users of such products—are at the implementation level. The prevalence of code-related problems, however, is a direct consequence of higher-level decisions to use programming languages, design methods, and libraries that admit these problems.

In systems where software failure could have significant human or financial costs, it is crucial that software be dependable—that it can be depended upon to function as expected and to not cause or contribute to adverse events in the environment in which it operates. Improvements in dependability would allow such systems to be used more widely and with greater confidence for the benefit of society. Moreover, software itself has great potential to bring improvements in safety in many areas.

Complete and reliable data about software-related system failures or the efficacy of particular software development approaches are hard to come by, making objective scientific evaluation difficult. Moreover, the lack of systematic reporting of software-related system failures is a serious problem that makes it more difficult to evaluate the risks and costs of such failures and to measure the effectiveness of proposed policies or interventions.

This lack of evidence has two direct consequences for this report. First, it has informed the key recommendations in this report regarding the need for evidence to be at the core of dependable software system development; for data collection efforts to be established; and for transparency and openness to be encouraged. Second, it has tempered the committee's desire to provide prescriptive guidance: The approach recommended is therefore largely free of endorsements or criticisms of particular development approaches, tools, or techniques. Moreover, the report leaves to the developers and procurers of individual systems the question of what level of dependability is appropriate, and what costs are worth incurring to achieve it.

Nonetheless, the evidence available to the committee did support several qualitative conclusions. First, developing software to meet even existing dependability criteria is difficult and costly. Large software projects fail at a high rate, and the cost of projects that do succeed in delivering highly dependable software is often exorbitant. Second, the quality of software produced by the industry is extremely variable, and there is inadequate oversight in some critical areas. Today's certification regimes and consensus standards have a mixed record. Some are largely ineffective, and some are counterproductive. They share a heavy reliance on testing, which cannot provide sufficient evidence for the high levels of dependability required in many critical applications.

A final observation is that the culture of an organization in which software is produced can have a dramatic effect on its quality and dependability. It seems likely that the excellent record of avionics software is due in large part to a safety culture in that industry that encourages meticulous attention to detail, high aversion to risk, and realistic assessment of software, staff, and process. Indeed, much of the benefit of standards such as DO-178B, Software Considerations in Airborne Systems and Equipment Certification, may be due to the safety culture that their strictures induce.

TOWARD CERTIFIABLY DEPENDABLE SOFTWARE

The focus of this report is a set of fundamental principles that underlie software system dependability and that suggest a different approach to the development and assessment of dependable software. Due to a lack of sufficient data to support or contradict any particular approach, a software system may not be declared "dependable" based on the method by which it was constructed. Rather, it should be regarded as dependable—certifiably dependable—only when adequate evidence has been marshaled in support of an argument for dependability that can be independently assessed. The goal of certifiably dependable software cannot therefore be achieved by mandating particular processes and approaches, regardless of their effectiveness in certain situations. Instead, software developers should marshal evidence to justify an explicit dependability claim that makes clear which properties in the real world the system is intended to establish. Such evidence forms a dependability case, and creating a dependability case is the cornerstone of the committee's approach to developing certifiably dependable software systems

Explicit Claims, Evidence, and Expertise

The committee's proposed approach can be summarized in "the three Cs"—explicit claims, evidence, and expertise:

- *Explicit claims.* No system can be "dependable" in all respects and under all conditions. So to be useful, a claim of dependability must be explicit. It must articulate precisely the properties the system is expected to exhibit and the assumptions about the system's environment upon which the claim is contingent. The claim should also indicate explicitly the level of dependability claimed, preferably in quantitative terms. Different properties may be assured to different levels of dependability.
- *Evidence.* For a system to be regarded as dependable, concrete evidence must be present that substantiates the dependability claim. This evidence will take the form of a dependability case arguing that the required properties follow from the combination of the properties of the system itself (that is, the implementation) and the environmental assumptions. Because testing alone is usually insufficient to establish properties, the case will typically combine evidence from testing with evidence from analysis. In addition, the case will inevitably involve appeals to the process by which the software was developed—for example, to argue that the software deployed in the field is the same software that was subjected to analysis or testing.

• *Expertise.* Expertise—in software development, in the domain under consideration, and in the broader systems context, among other things—is necessary to achieve dependable systems. Flexibility is an important advantage of the proposed approach; in particular the developer is not required to follow any particular process or use any particular method or technology. This flexibility allows experts freedom to employ new techniques and to tailor the approach to the system's application and domain. But the requirement to produce evidence is highly demanding and likely to stretch today's best practices to their limit. It will therefore be essential that developers are familiar with best practices and deviate from them only for good reason.

These prescriptions shape any particular development approach only in outline and give considerable freedom to developers in their choice of methods, languages, tools, and processes.

This approach is not, of course, a silver bullet. There are no easy solutions to the problem of developing dependable software, and there will always be systems that cannot be built to the required level of dependability even using the latest methods. But, the approach recommended is aimed at producing certifiably dependable systems today, and the committee believes it holds promise for developing the systems that will be needed in the future.

In the overall context of engineering, the basic tenets of the proposed approach are not controversial, so it may be a surprise to some that the approach is not already commonplace. Nor are the elements of the approach novel; they have been applied successfully for more than a decade. Nevertheless, this approach would require radical changes for most software development organizations and is likely to demand expertise that is currently in short supply.

Systems Engineering Approach

Complementing "the three *E*s" are several systems engineering ideas that provide an essential foundation for the building of dependable software systems:

• *Systems thinking.* Engineering fields with long experience in building complex systems (for example, aerospace, chemical, and nuclear engineering) have developed approaches based on "systems thinking." These approaches focus on properties of the system as a whole and on the interactions among its components, especially those interactions (often neglected) between a component being constructed and the components of its environment. As software has come to be deployed in—indeed has enabled—increasingly complex systems, the system aspect has come to dominate in questions of software dependability.

• *Software as a system component.* Dependability is not an intrinsic property of software. The committee strongly endorses the perspective of systems engineering, which views the software as one engineered artifact in a larger system of many components, some engineered and some given, and views the pursuit of dependability as a balancing of costs and benefits and a prioritization of risks. A software component that may be dependable in the context of one system might not be dependable in the context of another.

• *Humans as components.* People—the operators and users (and even the developers and maintainers) of a system—may also be viewed as system components. If a system meets its dependability criteria only if people act in certain ways, then those people should be regarded as part of the system, and an estimate of the probability that they will behave as required should be part of the evidence for dependability.

• *Real-world properties.* The properties of interest to the user of a system are typically located in the physical world: that a radiotherapy machine deliver a certain dose, that a telephone transmit a sound wave faithfully, that a printer make appropriate ink marks on paper, and so on. The software, on the other hand, is typically specified in terms of properties at its interfaces, which usually involve phenomena that are not of direct interest to the user: that the radiotherapy machine, telephone, or printer send or receive certain signals at certain ports, with the inputs related to the outputs according to some rules. It is important, therefore, to distinguish the requirements of a software system, which represent these properties in the physical world, from the specification of a software system, which characterizes the behavior of the software system at its interface with the environment. When the software system is itself only one component of a larger system, the other components in the system (including perhaps, as explained above, the people who work with the system) will be viewed as part of the environment. The dependability properties of a software system, therefore, should be expressed as requirements, and the dependability case should demonstrate how these properties follow from the combination of the specification and the environmental assumptions.

Coping with Complexity

The need for evidence of dependability and the difficulty of producing such evidence for complex systems have a straightforward but profound implication. Any component for which compelling evidence of dependability has been amassed at reasonable cost will likely be small by the standards of most modern software systems. Every critical specification property, therefore, will have to be assured by one, or at most a few, small components. Sometimes it will not be possible to separate concerns so cleanly, and in that case, the dependability case may be less credible or more expensive to produce.

As a result, one key to achieving dependability at reasonable cost is a serious and sustained commitment to simplicity, including simplicity of critical functions and simplicity in system interactions. This commitment is often the mark of true expertise. An awareness of the need for simplicity usually comes only with bitter experience and the humility gained from years of practice. There is no alternative to simplicity. Advances in technology or development methods will not make simplicity redundant; on the contrary, they will give it greater leverage. To achieve high levels of dependability in the foreseeable future, striving for simplicity is likely to be by far the most cost-effective of all interventions. Simplicity is not easy or cheap, but its rewards far outweigh its costs.

The most important form of simplicity is that produced by independence, in which particular system-level properties are guaranteed by individual components much smaller than the system as a whole, which can preserve these properties despite failures in the rest of the system. Independence can be established in the overall design of the system, with the support of architectural mechanisms. Its effect is to dramatically reduce the cost of constructing a dependability case for a property, since only a relatively small part of the system needs to be considered.

Appropriate simplicity and independence cannot be accomplished without addressing the challenges of "interactive complexity" and "tight coupling." Both interactive complexity, where components may interact in unanticipated ways, and tight coupling, wherein a single fault cannot be isolated but brings about other faults that cascade through the system, are correlated with the likelihood of system failure. Software-intensive systems tend to have both attributes. Careful attention should therefore be paid to the risks of interactive complexity and tight coupling and the advantages of modularity, isolation, and redundancy. The interdependences among components of critical software systems should be analyzed to ensure that there is no fault propagation path from less critical components to more critical components, that modes of failure are well understood, and that failures are localized to the greatest extent possible. The reduction of interactive complexity and tight coupling can contribute not only to the improvement of system dependability but also to the development of evidence and analysis in the service of a dependability case.

Rigorous Process and Preserving the Chain of Evidence

Generating a dependability case after the fact, when a development is largely complete, might be possible in theory. But in practice, at least with today's technology, the costs of doing so would be high, and it will be practical to develop a dependability case only if the system is built with its construction in mind. Each step in developing the software needs to preserve the chain of evidence on which will be based the argument that the resulting system is dependable.

At the start, the domain and environmental assumptions and the required properties of the system should be made explicit; they should be expressed unambiguously and in a form that permits systematic analysis to ensure that there are no unresolvable conflicts between the required properties. Each subsequent stage of development should preserve the evidence chain—that these properties have been carried forward without being corrupted—so each form in which the requirements, design, or implementation is expressed should support analysis to permit checking that the required properties have been preserved. What is sufficient will vary with the required dependability, but preserving the evidence chain necessitates that the checks are carried out in a disciplined way, following a documented procedure, and leaving auditable records.

The Roles of Testing, Analysis, and Formal Methods

Testing is indispensable, and no software system can be regarded as dependable if it has not been extensively tested, even if its correctness has been proven mathematically. Testing may find flaws that elude analysis because it exercises the system in its entirety, whereas analysis must typically make assumptions about the execution platform, the external environment, and operator responses, any of which may turn out to be unwarranted. At the same time, it is important to realize that testing alone is rarely sufficient to establish high levels of dependability. It is erroneous to believe that a rigorous development process, in which testing and code review are the only verification techniques used, justifies claims of extraordinarily high levels of dependability. Some certification schemes, for example, associate higher safety integrity levels with more burdensome process prescriptions and imply that following the processes recommended for the highest integrity levels will ensure that the failure rate is minuscule. In the absence of a carefully constructed dependability case, such confidence is misplaced.

Because testing alone will not be sufficient for the foreseeable future, the dependability claim will also require evidence produced by analysis.

Moreover, because analysis links the software artifacts directly to the claimed properties, the analysis component of the dependability case will usually contribute confidence at a lower cost than testing for the highest levels of dependability. A dependability case will generally require many forms of analysis, including (1) the validation of environmental assumptions, use models, and fault models; (2) the analysis of fault tolerance measures against fault models; (3) schedulability analysis for temporal behaviors; (4) security analysis against attack models; (5) verification of code against module specifications; and (6) checking that modules in aggregate achieve appropriate system-level effects. These analyses will sometimes involve informal argument that is carefully reviewed; sometimes mechanical inference (as performed, for example, by "type checkers" that confirm that memory is used in a consistent way and that boundaries between modules are respected); and, sometimes, formal proof. Indeed, the dependability case for even a relatively simple system will usually require all of these kinds of analysis, and they will need to be fitted together into a coherent whole.

Traditional software development methods rely on human inspection and testing for validation and verification. Formal methods also use testing, but they employ notations and languages that are amenable to rigorous analysis, and they exploit mechanical tools for reasoning about the properties of requirements, specifications, designs, and code. Practitioners have been skeptical about the practicality of formal methods. Increasingly, however, there is evidence that formal methods can yield systems of very high dependability in a cost-effective manner, at least for small to medium-sized critical systems. Although formal methods are typically more expensive to apply when only low levels of dependability are required, the cost of traditional methods rises rapidly with the level of dependability and often becomes prohibitive. When a highly dependable system is required, therefore, a formal approach may be the most cost effective.

CERTIFICATION, TRANSPARENCY, AND ACCOUNTABILITY

A variety of certification regimes exist for software in particular application domains. For example, the Federal Aviation Authority (FAA) itself certifies new aircraft (and air-traffic management) systems that include software, and this certification is then relied on by the customers who buy and use the aircraft; the National Information Assurance Partnership (NIAP) licenses third-party laboratories to assess security software products for conformance to the Common Criteria. Some large organizations have their own regimes for certifying that the software products they buy meet the organization's quality criteria, and many software product manufacturers have their own criteria that each version of their product must pass before release.

Few, if any, existing certification regimes encompass the combination of characteristics recommended in this report—namely, explicit dependability claims, evidence for those claims, and a rigorous argument that demonstrates that the evidence is sufficient to establish the validity of the claims. To establish that a system is dependable will involve inspection and analysis of the dependability claim and the evidence offered in its support. Where the customer for the system is not able to carry out that work itself (for lack of time or lack of expertise) it may need to involve a third party whose judgment it can rely on to be independent of commercial pressures from the vendor. Certification can take many forms, from self-certification by the supplier at one extreme, to independent third-party certification by a licensed certification authority at the other. No single certification regime is suitable for all circumstances, so a suitable scheme should be chosen for each circumstance. Industry groups and professional societies should consider developing model certification schemes appropriate to their domains, taking account of the detailed recommendations in this report.

When choosing suppliers and products, customers and users can make informed judgments only if the claims are credible. Such claims are unlikely to be credible if the evidence underlying them is not transparent. Economists have established that if consumers cannot reliably observe quality before they buy, sellers may get little economic benefit from providing higher quality than their competitors, and overall quality can decline. Sellers are concerned about future sales, and "reputation effects" compel them to strive to maintain a minimum level of quality. If consumers rely heavily on branding, though, it becomes more difficult for new firms to enter the market, and quality innovations spread more slowly.

Those claiming dependability for their software should therefore make available the details of their claims, criteria, and evidence. To assess the credibility of such details effectively, an evaluator should be able to calibrate not only the technical claims and evidence but also the organization that produced them, because the integrity of the evidence chain is vital and cannot easily be assessed without supporting data. This suggests that in some cases data of a more general nature should be made available, including the qualifications of the personnel involved in the development; the track record of the organization in providing dependable software; and the process by which the software was developed. The willingness of a supplier to provide such data, and the clarity and integrity of the data that the supplier provides, will be a strong indication of its attitude to dependability.

Where there is a need to deploy software that satisfies a particular dependability claim, it should always be explicit who is accountable for any failure to achieve it. Such accountability can be made explicit in the purchase contract, or as part of certification of the software, or as part of a professional licensing scheme, or in other ways. Since no single solution will suit all the circumstances in which certifiably dependable software systems are deployed, accountability regimes should be tailored to particular circumstances. At present, it is common for software developers to disclaim, so far as possible, all liability for defects in their products, to a greater extent than customers and society expect from manufacturers in other industries. Clearly, no software should be considered dependable if it is supplied with a disclaimer that withholds the manufacturer's commitment to provide a warranty or other remedies for software that fails to meet its dependability claims. Determining the appropriate scale of remedies, however, was beyond the scope of this study and would require a careful analysis of benefits and costs, taking into account not only the legal issues but also the state of software engineering, the various submarkets for software, the economic impact, and the effect on innovation.

KEY FINDINGS AND RECOMMENDATIONS

Presented below are the committee's findings and recommendations, each of which is discussed in more detail in Chapter 4.

Findings

Improvements in software development are needed to keep pace with societal demands for software. Avoidable software failures have already been responsible for loss of life and for major economic losses. The quality of software produced by the industry is extremely variable, and there is inadequate oversight in several critical areas. More pervasive deployment of software in the civic infrastructure may lead to catastrophic failures unless improvements are made. Software has the potential to bring dramatic benefits to society, but it will not be possible to realize these benefits—especially in critical applications—unless software becomes more dependable.

More data are needed about software failures and the efficacy of development approaches. Assessment of the state of the software industry, the risks posed by software, and progress made is currently hampered by the lack of a coherent source of information about software failures.

Recommendations to Builders and Users of Software

Make the most of effective software development technologies and formal methods. A variety of modern technologies—in particular, safe programming languages, static analysis (analysis of software and source code done without actually executing the program), and formal methods—are likely to reduce the cost and difficulty of producing dependable software.

Follow proven principles for software development. The committee's proposed approach also includes adherence to the following principles:

- *Take a systems perspective.* Here the dependability of software is viewed not in terms of intrinsic properties (such as the incidence of bugs in the code) but rather in terms of the system as a whole, including interactions among people, process, and technology.
- *Exploit simplicity.* If dependability is to be achieved at reasonable cost, simplicity should become a key goal, and developers and customers must be willing to accept the compromises it entails.

Make a dependability case for a given system and context: evidence, explicitness, and expertise. A software system should be regarded as dependable only if sufficient evidence of its explicitly articulated properties is presented to substantiate the dependability claim. This approach gives considerable leeway to developers to use whatever practices are best suited to the problem at hand. In practice the challenges of developing dependable software are sufficiently great that developers will need considerable expertise, and they will have to justify any deviations from best practices.

Demand more transparency, so that customers and users can make more informed judgments about dependability. Customers and users can make informed judgments when choosing suppliers and products only if the claims, criteria, and evidence for dependability are transparent.

Make use of but do not rely solely on process and testing. Testing will be an essential component of a dependability case, but will not in general suffice, because even the largest test suites typically used will not exercise enough paths to provide evidence that the software is correct nor will it have sufficient statistical significance for the levels of confidence usually desired. Rigorous process is essential for preserving the chain of dependability evidence but is not per se evidence of dependability.

Base certification on inspection and analysis of the dependability claim and the evidence offered in its support. Because testing and process alone are insufficient, the dependability claim will require, in addition, evidence produced by other modes of analysis. Security certification in particular should go beyond functional testing of the security components of a system and assess the effectiveness of measures the developer took to prevent the introduction of security vulnerabilities.

Include security considerations in the dependability case. Security vulnerabilities can undermine the case made for dependability properties by violating assumptions about how components behave, about their interactions, or about the expected behavior of users. The dependability case must therefore account explicitly for security risks that might compromise its other aspects. It is also important to ensure that security certifications give meaningful assurance of resistance to attack. New security certification regimes are needed that can provide confidence that most attacks against certified products or systems will fail. Such regimes can be built by applying the other findings and recommendations of this report, with an emphasis on the role of the environment—in particular, the assumptions made about the potential actions of a hostile attacker and the likelihood that new classes of vulnerabilities will be discovered and new attacks developed to exploit them.

Demand accountability and make it explicit. Where there is a need to deploy certifiably dependable software, it should always be made explicit who or what is accountable, professionally and legally, for any failure to achieve the declared dependability.

Recommendations to Agencies and Organizations That Support Software Education and Research

The committee was not constituted or charged to recommend budget levels or to assess trade-offs between software dependability and other priorities. However, it believes that the increasing importance of software to society and the extraordinary challenge currently faced in producing software of adequate dependability provide a strong rationale for investment in education and research initiatives.

Place greater emphasis on dependability—and its fundamental underpinnings—in the high school, undergraduate, and graduate education of software developers. Many practitioners do not have an adequate appreciation of the software dependability issues discussed in this report, are not aware of the most effective development practices available today, or are not capable of applying them appropriately. Wider implementation of the committee's recommended approach, which goes beyond today's state of the practice, implies a need for further education and training activities.

Federal agencies that support information technology research and development should give priority to basic research to further software-enabled system dependability, emphasizing a systems perspective and evidence. In keeping with this report's approach, such research should emphasize a systems perspective and "the three *Es*" (explicit claims, evidence, and expertise) and should be informed by a systems view that attaches more importance to those advances that are likely to have an impact in a world of large systems interacting with other systems and operators in a complex physical environment and organizational context.

1

Assessment:
Software Systems and
Dependability Today

The software industry is, by most measures, a remarkable success. But it would be unwise to be complacent and assume that software is already dependable enough or that its dependability will improve without any special efforts.

Software dependability is a pressing concern for several reasons:

• Developing software to meet existing dependability criteria is notoriously difficult and expensive. Large software projects fail at a rate far higher than other engineering projects, and the cost of projects that deliver highly dependable software is often exorbitant.

• Software failures have caused serious accidents that resulted in death, injury, and large financial losses. Without intervention, the increasingly pervasive use of software may bring about more frequent and more serious accidents.

• Existing certification schemes that are intended to ensure the dependability of software have a mixed record. Some are largely ineffective, and some are counterproductive.

• Software has great potential to improve safety in many areas. Improvements in dependability would allow software to be used more widely and with greater confidence for the benefit of society.

This chapter discusses each of these issues in turn. It then discusses the committee's five observations that informed the report's recommendations and findings.

COST AND SCHEDULE CHALLENGES
IN SOFTWARE DEVELOPMENT

For many years, international surveys have consistently reported that less than 30 percent of commercial software development projects are finished on time and within budget and satisfy the business requirements. The exact numbers are hard to discern and subject to much discussion and disagreement, because few surveys publish their definitions, methodologies, or raw data. However, there is widespread agreement that only a small percentage of projects deliver the required functionality, performance, and dependability within the original time and cost estimate.

Software project failure has been studied quite widely by governments, consultancy companies, academic groups, and learned societies. Two such studies are one published by the Standish Group and another by the British Computer Society (BCS). The Standish Group reported that 28 percent of projects succeeded, 23 percent were cancelled, and 49 percent were "challenged" (that is, overran significantly or delivered limited functionality).[1] The BCS surveyed[2] 38 members of the BCS, the Association of Project Managers, and the Institute of Management, covering 1,027 projects in total. Of these, only 130, or 12.7 percent, were successful; of the successful projects, 2.3 percent were development projects, 18.2 percent maintenance projects, and 79.5 percent data conversion projects—yet development projects made up half the total projects surveyed. That means that of the more than 500 development projects included in the survey, only three were judged to have succeeded.

The surveys covered typical commercial applications, but applications with significant dependability demands ("dependable applications," for short) show similar high rates of cancellation, overrun, and in-service failure. For example, the U.S. Department of Transportation's Office of the Inspector General and the Government Accountability Office track the progress of all major FAA acquisition projects intended to modernize and add new capabilities to the National Airspace System. As of May 2005, of 16 major acquisition projects being tracked, 11 were over budget, with total cost growth greater than $5.6 billion; 9 had experienced schedule delays ranging from 2 to 12 years; and 2 had been deferred.[3] Software is cited as the primary reason for these problems.

---

[1]Robert L. Glass, 2005, "IT failure rates—70 percent or 10-15 percent?" *IEEE Software* 22(3):112.

[2]Andrew Taylor, 2001, "IT projects sink or swim," Based on author's M.B.A. dissertation, *BCS Review*.

[3]DOT, Office of the Inspector General, 2005, "Status of FAA's major acquisitions: Cost growth and schedule delays continue to stall air traffic modernization," Report Number AV-2005-061, May 26.

An Air Force project that has been widely studied and reported illustrates the difficulty of developing dependable software using the methods currently employed by industry leaders. The F/A-22 aircraft has been under development since 1986. Much of the slow pace of development has been attributed to the difficulty of making the complex software dependable.[4] The instability of the software has often been cited as a cause of schedule delays[5,6] and the loss of at least one test aircraft.[7] The integrated avionics suite for the F/A-22 is reported to have been redesigned as recently as August 2005 to improve stability, among other things.[8]

The similarly low success rates in both typical and dependable applications is unsurprising, because dependable applications are usually developed using methods that do not differ fundamentally from those used commercially. The developers of dependable systems carry out far more reviews, more documentation, and far more testing, but the underlying methods are the same. The evidence is clear: These methods cannot dependably deliver today's complex applications, let alone tomorrow's even more complex requirements.

It must not be forgotten that creating dependable software systems itself has economic consequences. Consider areas such as dynamic routing in air traffic control, where there are not only significant opportunities to improve efficiency and (arguably) safety, but also great risks if automated systems fail.

DISRUPTIONS AND ACCIDENTS DUE TO SOFTWARE

The growing pervasiveness and centrality of software in our civic infrastructure is likely to increase the severity and frequency of accidents that can be attributed to software. Moreover, the risk of a major catastrophe in which software failure plays a part is increasing, because the growth in complexity and invasiveness of software systems is not being matched by improvements in dependability.

Software has already been implicated in cases of widespread economic disruption, major losses to large companies, and accidents in which

---

[4]Michael A. Dornheim, 2005, "Codes gone awry," *Aviation Week & Space Technology*, February 28, p. 63.

[5]Robert Wall, 2003, "Code Red emergency," *Aviation Week & Space Technology*, June 9, pp. 35-36.

[6]General Accounting Office, 2003, "Tactical aircraft, status of the F/A-22 program: Statement of Allen Li, director, Acquisition and Sourcing Management," GAO-33-603T, April 2.

[7]U.S. Air Force, "Aircraft accident investigation," F/A-22 S/N 00-4014. Available online at <http://www.airforcetimes.com/content/editorial/pdf/af.exsum_f22crash_060805.pdf>.

[8]Stephen Trimble, 2005, "Avionics redesign aims to improve F/A-22 stability," *Flight International*, August 23.

hundreds of people have been killed. Accidents usually have multiple causes, and software is rarely the sole cause. But this is no comfort. On the contrary, software can (and should) reduce, rather than increase, the risks of system failures.

The economic consequences of security failures in desktop software have been severe to date. Several individual viruses and worms have caused events where damage was assessed at over $1 billion each—Code Red was assessed at $2.75 billion worldwide[9]—and two researchers have estimated that a worst-case worm could cause $50 billion in damage.[10] One must also consider the aggregated effect of minor loss and inconvenience inflicted on large numbers of people. In several incidents in the last few years, databases containing the personal information of thousands of individuals—such as credit card data—were breached. Security attacks on personal computers are now so prevalent that according to some estimates, a machine connected to the Internet without appropriate protection would be compromised in under 4 minutes,[11] less time than it takes to download up-to-date security patches.

In domains where attackers may find sufficient motivation, such as the handling of financial records or the management of critical infrastructures, and with the growing risk and fear of terrorism and the evolution of mass network attacks, security has become an important concern. For example, as noted elsewhere, in the summer of 2005, radiotherapy machines in Merseyside, England, and in Boston were attacked by computer viruses. It makes little sense to invest effort in ensuring the dependability of a system while ignoring the possibility of security vulnerabilities. A basic level of security—in the sense that a software system behaves properly even in the presence of hostile inputs from its environment—should be required of any software system that is connected to the Internet, used to process sensitive or personal data, or used by an organization for its critical business or operational functions.

Automation tends to reduce the probability of failure while increasing its severity because it is used to control systems when such control is beyond the capabilities of human operators without such assistance.[12]

---

[9]See *Computer Economics*, 2003, "Virus attack costs on the rise—Again," Figure 1. Available online at <http://www.computereconomics.com/article.cfm?id=873>.

[10]Nicholas Weaver and Vern Paxson, 2004, "A worst-case worm," Presented at the Third Annual Workshop on Economics and Information Security (WEIS04), March 13-14. Available online at <http://www.dtc.umn.edu/weis2004/weaver.pdf>.

[11]Gregg Keizer, 2004, "Unprotected PCs fall to hacker bots in just four minutes," *Tech Web*, November 30. Available online at <http://www.techweb.com/wire/security/54201306>.

[12]N. Sarter, D.D. Woods, and C. Billings, 1997, "Automation surprises," *Handbook of Human Factors/Ergonomics*, 2nd ed., G. Salvendy, ed., Wiley, New York. (Reprinted in N. Moray, ed., *Ergonomics: Major Writings*, Taylor & Francis, Boca Raton, Fla., 2004.)

Aviation, for example, is no exception, and current trends—superairliners, free flight, greater automation, reduced human oversight in air-traffic control, and so on—increase the potential for less frequent but more serious accidents. High degrees of automation can also reduce the ability of human operators to detect and correct mistakes. In air-traffic control, for example, there is a concern that the failure of a highly automated system that guides aircraft, even if detected before an accident occurs, might leave controllers in a situation beyond their ability to resolve, with more aircraft to consider, and at smaller separations than they can handle. There is also a legitimate concern that a proliferation of safety devices itself creates new risks. The traffic alert and collision avoidance system (TCAS), an onboard collision avoidance system now mandatory on all commercial aircraft,[13] has been implicated in at least one near miss.[14]

Hazardous Materials

The potential for the worst software catastrophes resulting in thousands of deaths lies with systems involving hazardous materials, most notably plants for nuclear power, chemical processing, storing liquefied natural gas, and other related storage and transportation facilities. Although software has not been implicated in disasters on the scale of those in Chernobyl[15] or Bhopal,[16] the combination of pervasive software and high risk is worrying. Software is used pervasively in plants for monitoring and control in distributed control systems (DCS) and supervisory control and data acquisition (SCADA) systems. According to the EPA,[17] 123 chemical plants in the United States could each expose more than a million people if a chemical release occurred, and a newspaper article reports that a plant in Tennessee gave a worst-case estimate of 60,000 people facing death or serious injury from a vapor cloud formed by an

---

[13]For more information on TCAS, see the FAA's "TCAS home page." Available online at <http://adsb.tc.faa.gov/TCAS.htm>.

[14]N. Sarter, D.D. Woods, and C. Billings, 1997, "Automation surprises," *Handbook of Human Factors/Ergonomics*, 2nd ed., G. Salvendy, ed., Wiley, New York. (Reprinted in N. Moray, ed., *Ergonomics: Major Writings*, Taylor & Francis, Boca Raton, Fla., 2004.)

[15]See the Web site "Chernobyl.info: The international communications platform on the long-term consequences of the Chernobyl disaster" at <http://www.chernobyl.info/>.

[16]See BBC News' "One night in Bhopal." Available online at <http://www.bbc.co.uk/bhopal>.

[17]See U.S. General Accounting Office, 2004, "Federal action needed to address security challenges at chemical facilities," Statement of John B. Stephenson before the Subcommittee on National Security, Emerging Threats, and International Relations, Committee on Government Reform, House of Representatives (GAO-04-482T), p. 3. Available online at <http://www.gao.gov/new.items/d04482t.pdf>.

accidental release of sulfur dioxide.[18] Railways already make extensive use of software for signaling and safety interlocks, and the use of software for some degree of remote control of petrochemical tanker trucks (e.g., remote shutdown in an emergency) is being explored.[19]

Aviation

Smaller but still major catastrophes involving hundreds rather than thousands of deaths have been a concern primarily in aviation. Commercial flight is far safer than other means of travel, and the accident rate per takeoff and landing, or per mile, is extremely small (although accident rates in private and military aviation are higher). Increasing density of airspace use and the development of airliners capable of carrying larger numbers of passengers pose greater risks, however.

Although software has not generally been directly blamed for an aviation disaster, it has been implicated in some accidents and near misses. The 1997 crash of a Korean Airlines 747 in Guam resulted in 200 deaths and would almost certainly have been avoided had a minimum safe altitude warning system been configured correctly.[20] Several aircraft accidents have been attributed to "mode confusion," where the software operated as designed but not as expected by the pilots.[21] Several incidents in 2005 further illustrate the risks posed by software:

• In February 2005, an Airbus A340-642 en route from Hong Kong to London suffered from a failure in a data bus belonging to a computer that monitors and controls fuel levels and flow. One engine lost power and a second began to fluctuate; the pilot diverted the aircraft and landed safely in Amsterdam. The subsequent investigation noted that although a backup slave computer was available that was working correctly, the failing computer remained selected as the master due to faulty logic in the software. A second report recommended an independent low-fuel warning system and noted the risks of a computerized management system

---

[18]See James V. Grimaldi and Guy Gugliotta, 2001, "Chemical plants feared as targets," *Washington Post*, December 16, p. A01.

[19]See "Tanker truck shutdown via satellite," 2004, *GPS News*, November. Available online at <http://www.spacedaily.com/news/gps-03zn.html>.

[20]For more information, see the National Transportation Safety Board's formal report on the accident. Available online at <http://www.ntsb.gov/Publictn/2000/AAR0001.htm>.

[21]See NASA's "FM program: Analysis of mode confusion." Available online at <http://shemesh.larc.nasa.gov/fm/fm-now-mode-confusion.html>; updated August 6, 2001.

that might fail to provide crew with appropriate data, preventing them from taking appropriate actions.[22]

• In August 2005, a Boeing 777-200 en route from Perth to Kuala Lumpur presented the pilot with contradictory reports of airspeed: that the aircraft was overspeed and at the same time at risk of stalling. The pilot disconnected the autopilot and attempted to descend, but the auto-throttle caused the aircraft to climb 2,000 ft. He was eventually able to return to Perth and land the aircraft safely. The incident was attributed to a failed accelerometer. The air data inertial reference unit (ADIRU) had recorded the failure of the device in its memory, but because of a software flaw, the unit failed to recheck the device's status after power cycling.[23]

• In October 2005, an Airbus A319-131 flying from Heathrow to Budapest suffered a loss of cockpit power that shut down not only avionics systems but even the radio and transponder, preventing the pilot from issuing a Mayday call. At the time of writing, the cause has not been determined. An early report in the subsequent investigation noted, however, that an action was available to the pilots that would have restored power, but it was not shown on the user interface due to its position on a list, and a software design that would have required items higher on the list to be manually cleared in order for that available action to be shown.[24]

Perhaps the most serious software-related near miss incident to date occurred on September 14, 2004. A software system at the Los Angeles Air Route Traffic Control Center in Palmdale, California, failed, preventing any voice communication between controllers and aircraft. The center is responsible for aircraft flying above 13,000 ft in a wide area over southern California and adjacent states, and the outage disrupted about 800 flights across the country. According to the *New York Times*, aircraft violated minimum separation distances at least five times, and it was only due to onboard collision detection systems (i.e., TCAS systems) that no collisions actually occurred. The problem was traced to a bug in the software, in which a countdown timer reaching zero shut down the system.[25] The

---

[22]See Air Accidents Investigation Branch (AAIB) Bulletin S1/2005–SPECIAL (Ref: EW/C2005/02/03). Available online at <http://www.aaib.dft.gov.uk/cms_resources/G-VATL_Special_Bulletin1.pdf>.

[23]See Aviation Safety Investigation Report—Interim Factual, Occurrence Number 200503722. November 2006. Available online at <http://www.atsb.gov.au/publications/investigation_reports/2005/AAIR/aair200503722.aspx>.

[24]See AAIB Bulletin S3/2006 SPECIAL (Ref. EW/C2005/10/05). Available online at <http://www.aaib.dft.gov.uk/cms_resources/S3-2006%20G-EUOB.pdf>.

[25]L. Geppert, 2004, "Lost radio contact leaves pilots on their own," *IEEE Spectrum* 41(11):16-17.

presence of the bug was known, and the FAA was in the process of distributing a patch. The FAA ordered the system to be restarted every 30 days in the interim, but this directive was not followed. Worryingly, a backup system that should have taken over also failed within a minute of its activation. This incident, in common with the hospital system failure described in the next section, illustrates the greater risk that is created when services affecting a large area or many people are centralized in a single system, which then becomes a single point of failure.

Medical Devices and Systems

Medical devices such as radiation therapy machines and infusion pumps are potentially lethal. Implanted devices pose a particular threat, because although a single failure affects only one user, a flaw in the software of a device could produce failures across the entire population of users. Safety recalls of pacemakers and implantable cardioverter-defibrillators due to firmware (that is, software) problems between 1990 and 2000 affected over 200,000 devices, comprising 41 percent of the devices recalled and are increasing in frequency.[26] In the 20-year period from 1985 to 2005, the FDA's Maude database records almost 30,000 deaths and almost 600,000 injuries from device failures.[27]

In a study the FDA conducted between 1992 and 1998, 242 out of 3,140 device recalls (7.7 percent) were found to be due to faulty software.[28] Of these, 192—almost 80 percent—were caused by defects introduced during software maintenance.[29] The actual incidence of failures in medical devices due to software is probably much higher than these numbers suggest, as evidenced by a GAO study[30] that found extensive underreporting of medical device failures in general.

---

[26]William H. Maisel, Michael O. Sweeney, William G. Stevenson, Kristin E. Ellison, Laurence M. Epstein, 2001, "Recalls and safety alerts involving pacemakers and implantable cardioverter-defibrillator generators," *Journal of the American Medical Association* 286:793-799.

[27]FDA, 2006, *Ensuring the Safety of Marketed Medical Devices: CDRH's Medical Device Post-market Safety Program*. January.

[28]Insup Lee and George Pappas, 2006, *Report on the High-Confidence Medical-Device Software and Systems (HCMDSS) Workshop*. Available online at <http://rtg.cis.upenn.edu/hcmdss/HCMDSS-final-report-060206.pdf>.

[29]In addition, it should be noted that delays in vendor testing and certification of patches often make devices (and therefore even entire networks) susceptible to worms and other malware.

[30]GAO, 1986, "Medical devices: Early warning of problems is hampered by severe underreporting," U.S. Government Printing Office, Washington, D.C., GAO publication PEMD-87-1. For example, the study noted that of over 1,000 medical device failures surveyed, 9 percent of which caused injury and 37 percent of which had the potential to cause death or serious injury, only 1 percent were reported to the FDA.

Indeed, software failures have been responsible for some notable catastrophic device failures, of which perhaps the best known are failures associated with radiotherapy machines that led to patients receiving massive overdoses. The well-documented failure of the Therac-25, which led to more than five deaths between 1985 and 1987, exposed not only incompetence in software development but also a development culture unaware of safety issues.[31] A very similar accident in Panama in 2001[32] suggests that these lessons were not universally applied.[33]

As software becomes more pervasive in medicine, and reliance is placed not only on the software that controls physical processes but also on the results produced by diagnostic and scanning devices, the opportunity for software failures with lethal consequences will grow. In addition, software used for data management, while often regarded as noncritical, may in fact pose risks to patients that are far more serious than those posed by physical devices. Most hospitals are centralizing patient records and moving toward a system in which all records are maintained electronically. The failure of a hospital-wide database brings an entire hospital to a standstill, with catastrophic potential. Such failures have already been reported.[34]

An incident reported by Cook and O'Connor is indicative of the kinds of risks faced. A software failure in a pharmacy database in a tertiary-care hospital in the Chicago area made all medication records inaccessible

---

[31]See Nancy Leveson and Clark S. Turner, 1993, "An investigation of the Therac-25 accidents," *IEEE Computer* 26(7):18-41.

[32]See International Atomic Energy Agency (IAEA), 2001, "Investigation of an accidental exposure of radiotherapy patients in Panama: Report of a team of experts," International Atomic Energy Agency, Vienna, Austria. Available online at <http://www-pub.iaea.org/MTCD/publications/PDF/Pub1114_scr.pdf>.

[33]A number of studies have investigated challenges related to infusion devices. See R.I. Cook, D.D. Woods, and M.B. Howie, 1992, "Unintentional delivery of vasoactive drugs with an electromechanical infusion device," *Journal of Cardiothoracic and Vascular Anesthesia* 6:238-244; M. Nunnally, C.P. Nemeth, V. Brunetti, and R.I. Cook, 2004, "Lost in menuspace: User interactions with complex medical devices," *IEEE Transactions on Systems, Man and Cybernetics—Part A: Systems and Humans* 34(6):736-742; L. Lin, R. Isla, K. Doniz, H. Harkness, K. Vicente, and D. Doyle, 1998, "Applying human factors to the design of medical equipment: Patient controlled analgesia," *Journal of Clinical Monitoring* 14:253-263; L. Lin, K. Vicente, and D.J. Doyle, 2001, "Patient safety, potential adverse drug events, and medical device design: A human factors engineering approach," *Journal of Biomedical Informatics* 34(4):274-284; R.I. Cook, D.D. Woods, and C. Miller, 1998, *A Tale of Two Stories: Contrasting Views on Patient Safety*, National Patient Safety Foundation, Chicago, Ill., April. Available online at <http://www.npsf.org/exec/report.html>.

[34]See, for example, Peter Kilbridge, 2003, "Computer crash: Lessons from a system failure," *New England Journal of Medicine* 348:881-882, March 6; Richard Cook and Michael O'Connor, "Thinking about accidents and systems," forthcoming, in K. Thompson and H. Manasse, eds., *Improving Medication Safety*, American Society of Health-System Pharmacists, Washington, D.C.

for almost a day. The pharmacy relied on this database for selecting and distributing medications throughout the hospital and was only able to continue to function by collecting paper records from nurses' stations and reentering all the data manually. Had the paper records not been available, the result would have been catastrophic. Although no patients were injured, Cook and O'Connor were clear about the significance of the event: "Accidents are signals sent from deep within the systems about the sorts of vulnerability and potential for disaster that lie within."[35]

In many application areas, effectiveness and safety are clearly distinguished from each other. In medicine, however, the distinction can be harder to make. The accuracy of the data produced by medical information systems is often critical, and failure to act in a timely fashion can be as serious as failure to prevent an accident. Moreover, the integration of invasive devices with hospital networks will ultimately erase the gap between devices and databases, so that failures in seemingly unimportant back-office applications might compromise patient safety. Networking also makes hospital systems vulnerable to security attacks; in the summer of 2005, radiotherapy machines in Merseyside, England[36] were attacked by a computer virus. In contrast to the problem described above, this attack affected availability, not the particular treatment delivered.

Computerized physician order entry (CPOE) systems are widely used and can reduce the incidence of medical errors as well as bring efficiency improvements. The ability to take notes by computer rather than by hand and instantly make such information available to others of the medical team can save lives. The ability to record prescriptions the minute they are prescribed, and the automated checking of these prescriptions against others the patient is taking, reduces the likelihood of interactions. The ability to make a tentative diagnosis and instantly receive information on treatment options clearly improves efficiency. But one study[37] suggests that poorly designed and implemented systems can actually facilitate medication errors. User interfaces may be poorly designed and hard to use, and important functions that once, before computerization, were implemented by other means may be missing. Moreover, users can

---

[35]Richard Cook and Michael O'Connor, "Thinking about accidents and systems," forthcoming, in K. Thompson and H. Manasse, eds., *Improving Medication Safety*, American Society of Health-System Pharmacists, Washington, D.C., p. 15. Available online at <http://www.ctlab.org/documents/ASHP_chapter.pdf>.

[36]BBC News, 2005, "Hospital struck by computer virus," August 22. Available online at <http://news.bbc.co.uk/1/hi/england/merseyside/4174204.stm>.

[37]Ross Koppel, Joshua P. Metlay, Abigail Cohen, Brian Abaluck, A. Russell Localio, Stephen E. Kimmel, and Brian L. Strom, 2005, "Role of computerized physician order entry systems in facilitating medication errors," *Journal of the American Medical Association* 293(10):1197-1203.

become reliant on the information such systems provide, even to the point of using it for invalid purposes (for example, using doses in the pharmacy database to infer normative ranges).

The usability of medical information systems is an important consideration as poor usability may not only lead to accidents but may also reduce or even eliminate efficiency gains and lower the quality of care. If an information system is not designed to carefully represent complex traditional procedures in digital form, information may be lost or misrepresented. Moreover, avenues for data entry by physicians need to ensure that the physicians are able to pay sufficient attention to the patient and pick up any subtle cues about the illness without being distracted by the computer and data entry process.

Many of these challenges might stem from organizational control issues—centralized and rigid design that fails to recognize the nature of practice,[38] central rule-making designed to limit clinical choices, insurance requirements that bin various forms of a particular condition in a way that fails to individualize treatment, and insufficient assessment after deployment. However, technology plays a role in poorly designed and inefficient user interfaces as well. Although the computerization of health care can offer improvements in safety and efficiency, care is needed so that computerization does not undermine the safety of existing manual procedures. In the medical device industry, for example, while many of the largest manufacturers have well-established safety programs, smaller companies may face challenges with respect to safety, perhaps because they lack the necessary resources and expertise.[39]

Infrastructure

By enhancing communication and live data analysis, software offers opportunities for efficiency improvements in transportation and other infrastructure. Within a decade or two, for example, traffic flow may be controlled by extensive networks of monitors, signals, and traffic advisories sent directly to cars.[40] A major, sustained failure of such a system might be catastrophic. For critical functions such as ambulance, fire, and police services, any failure has catastrophic potential. The failure of even

---

[38]See Kathryn Montgomery, 2006, *How Doctors Think, Clinical Judgment and the Practice of Medicine*, Oxford University Press, Oxford, United Kingdom.

[39]A recent FDA report estimates that there are about 15,000 manufacturers of medical devices and notes that "these small firms may lack the experience to anticipate, recognize, or address manufacturing problems that may pose safety concerns." *Ensuring the Safety of Marketed Medical Devices: CDRH's Medical Device Postmarket Safety Program*, January 2006.

[40]See ongoing work at <http://www.foresight.gov.uk/Intelligent_Infrastructure_Systems/Index.htm>.

one component, such as the dispatch system, can have significant reper-
cussions; the infamous collapse of the London Ambulance System[41] demonstrated how vulnerable such a system is just to failures of availability.

Software is a key enabler for greater fuel efficiency; modern cars rely
heavily on software for engine control, and in some cars, control is largely
by electrical rather than mechanical means. However, software flaws might
cause a car to fail to respond to commands or even to shut down entirely.
Whereas mechanical failures are often predictable (through evidence of
wear, for example), software failures can be sudden and unexpected and,
due to coupling, can have far-reaching effects. In 2005, for example, Toyota
identified a software flaw that caused Prius hybrid cars to stall or shut
down when traveling at high speed; 23,900 vehicles were affected.[42]

In the realm of communications infrastructure, advances in telecommunications have resulted in lower costs, greater flexibility, and huge
increases in bandwidth. These improvements have not, however, been
accompanied by improvements in robustness. Cell phone networks have
a different—not necessarily improved—vulnerability posture than conventional landline systems, and even the Internet, despite its redundan-
cies, may be susceptible to failure under extreme load.[43] The disaster on
September 11 and Hurricane Katrina were both exacerbated by failures of
communication systems.[44]

Defense

The U.S. military is a large, if not the largest, user of information technology and software. Failures in military systems, as one might expect,
can have disastrous consequences:

> A U.S. soldier in Afghanistan used a Precision Lightweight GPS Re-
> ceiver—a "plugger"—to set coordinates for an air strike. He then saw

---

[41]D. Page, P. Williams, and D. Boyd, 1993, *Report of the Inquiry into the London Ambulance Service*, Communications Directorate, South West Thames Regional Health Authority, London, February. Available online at <http://www.cs.ucl.ac.uk/staff/
A.Finkelstein/las/lascase0.9.pdf>.

[42]Sholnn Freeman, 2005, "Toyota attributes Prius shutdowns to software glitch,"
Wall Street Journal, May 16. Available online at <http://online.wsj.com/article_print/
SB111619464176634063.html>.

[43]For a discussion of how the traditional landline phone system and the Internet manage congestion and other issues, see National Research Council, 1999, *Trust in Cyberspace*,
National Academy Press, Washington, D.C. Available online at <http://books.nap.edu/
catalog.php?record_id=6161>.

[44]For more information on communications relating to September 11, 2001, see National
Research Council, 2003, *The Internet Under Crisis Conditions: Learning from September 11*, The
National Academies Press, Washington, D.C. Available online at <http://books.nap.edu/
catalog.php?record_id=10569>.

that the "battery low" warning light was on. He changed the battery, then pressed "Fire." The device was designed, on starting or resuming operation after a battery change, to initialize the coordinate variables to its own location.[45]

It was reported that three soldiers were killed in this incident.[46] The error appears to have been the result of failing to consider the larger system when defining the safety properties that guided the design of the software. Hazard analysis should have revealed the danger of transmitting the location of the plugger as the destination for a missile strike, and once the hazard had been identified, it would be straightforward to specify a system property that required (for example) that the specified target be more than some specified (safe) distance away, and that this be checked by the software before the target coordinates are transmitted.

Defense systems with high degrees of automation are inherently risky. The Patriot surface-to-air missile, for example, failed with catastrophic effect on several occasions. An Iraqi Scud missile hit the U.S. barracks in Dhahran, Saudi Arabia, in February 1991, killing 28 soldiers; a government investigation[47] found that a Patriot battery failed to intercept the missile because of a software error. U.S. Patriot missiles downed a British Tornado jet and an American F/A-18 Hornet in the Iraq war in 2003.

Distribution of Energy and Goods

Software failures could also interrupt the distribution of goods and services, such as gasoline, food, and electricity. An extended blackout during wintertime in a cold area of the United States would be an emergency. The role of software in the blackout in the Northeast in 2003 is complicated, but at the very least it seems clear that had the software monitoring system correctly identified the initial overload, it could have been contained without leading to systemwide failure.[48]

Apart from experiencing functional failures or design flaws, software is also vulnerable to malicious attacks. The very openness and ubiquity that makes networked systems attractive exposes them to attack by van-

---

[45]From page 83 in Michael Jackson, 2004, "Seeing more of the world," *IEEE Software* 21(6):83-85. Available online at <http://mcs.open.ac.uk/mj665/SeeMore3.pdf>.

[46]Vernon Loeb, 2002, "'Friendly fire' deaths traced to dead battery: Taliban targeted, but US forces killed," *Washington Post*, March 24, p. A21.

[47]GAO, 1992, *Patriot Missile Software Problem*, Report of the Information Management and Technology Division. Available online at <http://www.fas.org/spp/starwars/gao/im92026.htm>.

[48]See Charles Perrow, 2007, *The Next Catastrophe: Reducing our Vulnerabilities to Natural, Industrial, and Terrorist Disasters*, Princeton University Press, Princeton, N.J., Chapter 7.

dals or criminals. The trend to connecting critical systems to the Internet is especially worrying, because it often involves placing in a new and unknown environment a program whose design assumed that it would be running on an isolated computer. In the summer of 2005, two separate incidents were reported wherein radiotherapy systems were taken offline because their computers were infected by viruses after the systems had been connected to the Internet.[49] Numerous studies and significant research have been carried out in software and network security. This report does not focus on the security aspects of dependability, but analysis of the security aspects of a system should be part of any dependability case (see Chapter 2 for a discussion of dependability cases generally, and see Chapter 3 for more on security).

Voting

There have been many reports of failures of software used for electronic voting, although none have been substantiated by careful and objective analysis. But there are few grounds for confidence, and some of the most widely used electronic voting software has been found by independent researchers to be insecure and of low quality.[50] In the 2006 election in Sarasota County, Florida, the outcome was decided by a margin of 363 votes, yet over 18,000 ballots cast on electronic voting machines did not register a vote. A lawsuit filed to force a revote cites, among other things, the possibility of software malfunction and alleges that the machines were improperly certified.[51]

PROBLEMS WITH EXISTING CERTIFICATION SCHEMES

Evidence for the efficacy of existing certification schemes is hard to come by. What seems certain, however, is that experience with certification varies dramatically across domains, with different communities of users, developers, and certifiers having very different perceptions of certification. A variety of certification regimes exist for software in particular application domains. For example, the Federal Aviation Authority (FAA) itself certifies new aircraft (and air-traffic management) systems that include software, and this certification is then relied on by the cus-

---

[49]BBC News, 2005, "Hospital struck by computer virus," August 25. Available online at <http://news.bbc.co.uk/1/hi/england/merseyside/4174204.stm>.

[50]See Avi Rubin et al., 2004, "Analysis of an electronic voting system," *IEEE Symposium on Security and Privacy*, Oakland, Calif., May. Available online at <http://avirubin.com/vote.pdf>.

[51]See the full complaint online at <http://www.eff.org/Activism/E-voting/florida/sarasota_complaint.pdf>.

tomers who buy and use the aircraft; whereas the National Information Assurance Partnership (NIAP) licenses third-party laboratories to assess security software products for conformance to the Common Criteria (CC).[52] Some large organizations have their own regimes for certifying that the software products they buy meet their quality criteria, and many product manufacturers have their own criteria that each version of their product must pass before release. Few, if any, existing certification regimes encompass the combination of characteristics recommended in this report: namely, explicit dependability claims, evidence for those claims, and a demand for expertise sufficient to construct a rigorous argument that demonstrates that the evidence is sufficient to establish the validity of the claims.

On the one hand, in the domain of avionics software, the certification process (and the culture that surrounds it) is held in high regard and is credited by many for an excellent safety record, with software implicated in only a handful of incidents. On the other hand, in the domain of software security, certification has been a dismal failure: New security vulnerabilities appear daily, and certification schemes are regarded by developers as burdensome and ineffective.

Security Certification

Security certification standards for software were developed initially in response to the needs of the military for multilevel-secure products that could protect classified information from disclosure. Concern for security in computing is now universal. The most widely recognized security certification standard is the CC. In short, since CC is demanded by some government agencies, it is widely applied; however better criteria would make it more effective and less burdensome.

Like its predecessors, the CC is a process in which independent government-accredited evaluators conduct technical analyses of the security properties of—typically—commercial off-the-shelf (COTS) IT products and then certify the presence and quality of those properties. The CC model allows end users or government agencies to write a protection profile that specifies attributes of the security features of a product (such as the granularity of access controls and the level of detail captured in audit

---

[52]CC was finalized in the late 1990s by the national governments that are signatories to the Common Criteria Mutual Recognition Agreement. It succeeds the U.S. Trusted Computer Systems Evaluation Criteria (TCSEC, or Orange Book) and the European IT Security Evaluation Criteria. The description in the next section is simplified but fundamentally accurate. It is based on presentations to the committee and on discussions of CC at the Common Criteria Users' Forum in Washington, D.C., October 2004.

logs) and the level of security assurance of a product, as determined by the quality of its design and implementation.

The CC characterizes assurance at one of seven levels, referred to as Evaluation Assurance Levels or EAL 1 (the lowest) through 7 (the highest). Each higher EAL requires more structured design documentation (and presumably more structured design), more detailed documentation, more extensive testing, and better control over the development environment. At the three highest levels of assurance (EALs 5-7), formal specification of system requirements, design, or implementation is mandated.

With a handful of exceptions,[53] COTS products complete evaluations only at the lowest four levels of assurance (EALs 1-4). Commercial vendors of widely used software have not committed either to the use of formal methods or to the extensively documented design processes that the higher levels of the CC require. Typical vendor practice for completing evaluation is to hire a specialized contractor who reviews whatever documentation the vendor's process has produced as well as the product source code and then produces the documentation and associated tests that the CC requires. The vendor often has the option of excluding problematic features (and code) from the "evaluated configuration." A separate contractor team of evaluators (often another department of the company that produces the evidence) then reads the documentation and reviews the test plans and test results. At EALs 1-4, the assurance levels applied to COTS products, the evaluators may conduct a penetration test to search for obvious vulnerabilities or at the Enhanced Basic level for other flaws (both criteria as defined in the CC documents).[54] If the evaluators find that all is in order, they recommend that the responsible government agency grant CC certification to the product as configured. In the United States, the National Security Agency employs validators who are government employees or consultants with no conflicts of interest to check the work of the evaluators.

Because the CC certification process focuses on documentation designed to meet the needs of the evaluators, it is possible for a product to complete CC evaluation even though the evaluators do not have a deep understanding of how the product functions. And because the certification process at economically feasible evaluation levels focuses on the functioning of the product's security features even while real vulnerabilities can occur in any component or interface, real-world vulnerability

---

[53]The smartcard industry has embraced higher levels of evaluation, and many smartcard products have completed evaluation at EAL 5. Of more than 400 evaluated products other than smartcards listed at <http://www.commoncriteriaportal.org>, only 7 have completed evaluation at EAL 5 or higher.

[54]See CC *Evaluation Methodology* manuals versions 2.3 and 3.1, respectively.

data show that products that have undergone evaluation fare no better (and sometimes worse) than products that have not.[55]

While the CC evaluation of security features gives users some confidence that the features are appropriate and consistent, most users would logically assume that a product that had completed evaluation would have fewer vulnerabilities (cases in which an attacker could defeat the product's security) than a product that had not been evaluated. Sadly, there is no evidence that this is the case.

CC evaluation does not necessarily correlate with the observed rate of vulnerability, as the following examples illustrate. The first example, which a member of the committee participated in at Microsoft, considers the relative effectiveness of CC evaluation and other measures in reducing security vulnerabilities in two Microsoft operating system versions. Microsoft's Windows 2000 was evaluated at the highest evaluation level usually sought by commercial products (EAL 4), a process that cost many millions of dollars and went on for roughly 3 years after Windows 2000 had been released to customers. However, Windows 2000, as fielded, experienced a large number of security vulnerabilities both before and after the evaluation was completed. A subsequent Windows version, Windows Server 2003, was subject to an additional series of pragmatic steps such as threat modeling and application of static analysis tools during its development. These steps proved effective, with the result that the (then-unevaluated) Windows Server 2003 experienced about half the rate of critical vulnerabilities in the field as its CC-evaluated predecessor.[56] Some 18 months later, a CC evaluation against the same set of requirements as for Windows 2000 was completed for Windows Server 2003. The evaluation was useful insofar as it demonstrated the operating system contained a relatively complete set of security features, However, Microsoft's assessment was that the vulnerability rate of Windows Server 2003 was better than that of Windows 2000 because of a reduced incidence of errors at the coding level, a level well below the level at which it is scrutinized by the CC evaluation. Another example is a recent comparison[57] of the vulnerability rates of database products, which indicated that a product

---

[55]See, for example, the National Vulnerability Database online at <http://nvd.nist.gov/> and a list of evaluated products at <http://www.commoncriteriaportal.org/public/consumer/index.php?menu=5>.

[56]For information on security vulnerabilities and fixes, see the Microsoft Security Bulletin Web site at <http://www.microsoft.com/technet/security/current.aspx>.

[57]See David Litchfield, 2006, "Which database is more secure? Oracle vs. Microsoft," an NGS Software Insight Security Research (NISR) publication. Available online at <http://www.databasesecurity.com/dbsec/comparison.pdf>. The National Vulnerability Database at <http://nvd.nist.gov/> also provides information on this topic.

that had completed several CC evaluations actually experienced a higher vulnerability rate than one that had completed none.

These data, and comparable data on other classes of products, demonstrate that completion of CC evaluations does not give users confidence that evaluated products will show lower vulnerability rates than products that have not been evaluated. While evaluation against a suitable protection profile ensures completeness and consistency of security features, most users would expect (incorrectly) that CC evaluation is an indicator of better security, which they equate with fewer vulnerabilities.

The problem with CC goes beyond the certification process itself. Its fundamental assumption is that security certification should focus on security components—namely, components that implement security features, such as access control. This is akin to evaluating the security of a building by checking the mechanisms of the door locks. Software attackers, like common burglars, more often look for weaknesses in overall security—for example, for entry points that are not guarded. In computer security jargon, an evaluation should consider the entire attack surface of the system. The CC community is well aware of these problems and has discussed them at length. Unfortunately, the newly released CC version 3 does not show any significant change of direction.

Avionics Certification

Avionics systems are not certified directly but are evaluated as part of the aircraft as a whole. In the United States, when the regulations governing aircraft design were initially developed, avionics systems were implemented in hardware alone and did not incorporate software. The introduction of software into civilian aircraft beginning in the 1970s exposed inadequacies in the regulations relating to avionics: They could not be readily applied to software-based systems. In 1980, a special committee (SC-145) of the Radio Technical Commission for Aeronautics (RTCA) was created to develop guidelines for evaluating software used on aircraft. It was composed of representatives of aircraft manufacturers and avionics manufacturers, members of the academic community, aircraft customers, and certifiers. The committee released its report, *Software Considerations in Airborne Systems and Equipment Certification* (RTCA DO-178), in 1982. The document was subsequently revised, and the present 1992 version, DO-178B, eventually became the de facto standard worldwide for software in civilian aircraft. In Europe, it is known as ED-12B and is published by the European equivalent of RTCA, the European Organisation for Civil Aviation Equipment (EUROCAE).[58]

---

[58]More information on the work of EUROCAE is available online at <http://www.eurocae.org/>.

DO-178B classifies software using the FAA's five failure levels to characterize the impact of that particular software's failure on an aircraft[59]—ranging from Level A (catastrophic) to Level E (no effect on the operational capability of an aircraft)—and prescribes more stringent criteria at higher levels. DO-178B tends to focus more on eliminating defects than on preventing their introduction in the first place. The desire to make DO-178B widely acceptable also made it imprecise, and evaluations have yielded very different results when conducted by different organizations or government agencies. For example, there are very few detailed requirements for standards and checklists contained within DO-178B. Where one evaluator may be satisfied to check against a set of criteria in a checklist or standard, another may document numerous deficiencies based on his or her own experience, and DO-178B cannot be used to adjudicate between the two different results.[60] A dearth of skilled personnel with a stable body of knowledge and capable of delivering consistent interpretations has exacerbated the situation. Evaluators were typically drawn from industry, but despite having good practical experience, they rarely had any formal qualifications in software engineering. To reduce variability, additional explanatory guidance and procedures were developed, and certifiers were given special training. These steps have led to a more prescriptive approach and have resulted in better standardization.

At least in comparison with other domains (such as medical devices), avionics software appears to have fared well inasmuch as major losses of life and severe injuries have been avoided. However, this is not in itself evidence that any or all of the processes prescribed by the DO-178B standard are necessary or cost effective. To give one example, DO-178B lays down criteria for structural coverage of the source code during testing depending on the criticality of the component. The unstated purpose is to establish that requirements-based testing has ensured that all source code has been completely exercised with a rigor commensurate with the hazard associated with the software. Without considerable negotiation, no other approaches are allowable. However, in one published study, detailed analysis and comparison of systems that had been certified to Levels A or B of DO-178B showed that there was no discernible differ-

---

[59]Adapted from Jim Alves-Foss, Bob Rinker, and Carol Taylor, undated, "Merging safety and assurance: The process of dual certification for FAA and the Common Criteria." Available online at <http://www.csds.uidaho.edu/comparison/slides.pdf>.

[60]This was documented in the following NASA report: K.J. Hayhurst, C.A. Dorsey, J.C. Knight, N.G. Leveson, and G.F. McCormick, 1999, "Streamlining software aspects of certification: Report on the SSAC survey." NAS/TM-1999-209519, August, Section 3, observations 1, 3, 4, 5 (p. 45). The report is available online at <http://ntrs.nasa.gov/archive/nasa/casi.ntrs.nasa.gov/19990070314_1999110914.pdf>, and an overview of the SSAC process is available online at <http://shemesh.larc.nasa.gov/ssac/>.

ence between the two levels in the remaining level of anomalies in the software, and that these anomalies included many serious, safety-related defects.[61] The main difference between Level A (software that could lead to a catastrophic failure) and Level B (software whose failure would at most be severely hazardous) is that Level A calls for requirements-based testing to be shown to provide MCDC coverage of the software. This suggests that MCDC test coverage (at least as carried out on the software examined in the lessons learned study mentioned above[62]) does not significantly increase the probability of detecting any serious defects that remain in the software.

Medical Software Certification

Medical software, in contrast to avionics software, is generally not subject to uniform standards and certification. The Food and Drug Administration (FDA) evaluates new products in a variety of ways. Some are subject to premarket approval (PMA), which is "based on a determination by FDA that the PMA contains sufficient valid scientific evidence to assure that the device is safe and effective for its intended use(s)."[63] Other classes of products are subject to premarket notification, which requires manufacturers to demonstrate that the product is substantially equivalent to, or as safe and effective as, an existing product. The FDA's requirements for this procedure are minimal.[64] They center on a collection of guidance documents that outline the kinds of activities expected and suggest consensus standards that might be adopted. The larger manufacturers often voluntarily adopt a standard such as the International Electrotechnical Commission's (IEC's) 61508,[65] a standard related to the functional safety

---

[61] Andy German and Gavin Mooney, 2001, "Air vehicle software static code analysis—Lessons learnt," *Proceedings of the Ninth Safety-Critical Systems Symposium*, Felix Redmill and Tom Anderson, eds., Springer-Verlag, Bristol, United Kingdom.

[62] In the study cited above, few survey respondents found MCDC testing to be effective—it rarely revealed errors according to 59 percent and never revealed them at all according to 12 percent. That survey (which had a 72 percent response rate) also found that 76 percent of respondents acknowledged inconsistency between approving authorities; only 7 percent said that the guidance provided was ample (with 33 percent deeming it insufficient and 55 percent barely sufficient); and 75 percent found the cost and time for MCDC to be substantial or nearly prohibitive. The committee is not aware of results suggesting significant changes in the ensuing years.

[63] See the FDA's "Device advice" on premarket approval. Available online at <http://www.fda.gov/cdrh/devadvice/pma/>.

[64] The FDA's guidance on premarket notification is available online at <http://www.fda.gov/cdrh/devadvice/314.html>.

[65] For more information on IEC 61508, see <http://www.iec.ch/zone/fsafety/pdf_safe/hld.pdf>; for information on ISA S84.01, see <http://www.isa.org/>.

of electrical/electronic/programmable electronic-safety-related systems, or its U.S. equivalent, ISA S84.01. The certification process itself typically involves a limited evaluation of the manufacturer's software process.

The consensus standards contain a plethora of good advice and are mostly process-based, recommending a large collection of practices. They emphasize "verification" repeatedly, but despite the safety-critical nature of many of the devices to which they are applied, they largely equate verification with testing (which, as explained elsewhere in this report, is usually insufficient for establishing high dependability) and envisage no role for analysis beyond traditional reviews. The FDA's guidance document,[66] like the IEC's, has a lengthy section on testing techniques and discusses how the level of criticality should determine the level of testing. It recognizes the limitations of testing and suggests the use of other verification techniques to overcome these limitations, but it does not specify what these might be.

OPPORTUNITIES FOR DEPENDABLE SOFTWARE

Analyses of the role of software in safety-critical systems often focus on their potential to cause harm. It is important to balance concern about the risks of more pervasive software with a recognition of the enormous value that software brings, not only by improving efficiency but also by making systems safer. Software can reduce the risk of a system failure by monitoring for warning signs and controlling interventions; it can improve the quality and timeliness of information provided to operators; and it can oversee the activities of error-prone humans. Software can also enable a host of new applications, tools, and systems that can contribute to the health and well-being of the population.

Without better methods for developing dependable software, it may not be possible to build the systems we would like to build. When software is introduced into critical settings, the benefits must obviously outweigh the risks, and without convincing evidence that the risk of catastrophic failure is sufficiently low, society may be reluctant to field the system whatever the benefits may be. In the United States, the threat of litigation may raise the bar even higher, since failing to deploy a new system that improves safety is less likely to result in damage claims than deploying a system that causes injury.

To illustrate these issues, we consider the same two domains: air transportation and medicine.

---

[66]FDA, 2002, *General Principles of Software Validation; Final Guidance for Industry and FDA Staff*, January 11. Available online at <http://www.fda.gov/cdrh/comp/guidance/938.html>.

Air Transportation

Software already plays a critical role in air transportation, most notably in onboard avionics and in air-traffic management. Dependable software will be a linchpin of safe air transport in the coming decades, in two areas in particular.[67] First, efforts to enhance aviation functionality, such as plans for (1) new avionics systems that incorporate full-authority digital engine controllers (FADECs) to manage large engines and monitor their performance and (2) flight-deck and ground-based automation to support free flight, will rely heavily on software.

Second, there are efforts to improve aviation safety by employing automation in the detection and mitigation of accidents.[68] The category of accident responsible for most fatalities involving commercial jetliners is "controlled flight into terrain" (CFIT), in which the pilot, usually during takeoff or landing, inadvertently flies the aircraft into the ground. Collisions between planes during ground operations, takeoff, and landing also merit attention; a runway incursion in the Canary Islands in 1977 resulted in one of the worst accidents in aviation history, with 583 fatalities. While such accidents are not common, they pose significant risk.

Software can help prevent both kinds of accident, with—for example— ground proximity warning systems and automatic alerts for runway incursions. Software can also be used to defend against mechanical failures: the Aircraft Condition Analysis and Management System (ACAMS) uses onboard components and ground-based information systems to diagnose weaknesses and communicate them to maintainers.

Medicine

Software is crucial to the future of medicine. Although computers are already widely used in hospitals and doctors' offices, the potential benefits of IT in patient management have been garnering increased attention of late. The ready availability of information and automated record keeping can have an impact on health care that goes far beyond efficiency improvements. Each year, an estimated 98,000 patients die from preventable medical errors.[69] Many of these deaths could be prevented by software. CPOE systems, for example, can dramatically reduce the rate

---

[67] This section is based on information provided in John C. Knight, 2002, "Software challenges in aviation systems," *Lecture Notes in Computer Science* 2434:106-112.

[68] See, for example, the NASA Aviation Safety Program. Available online at <http://www.aerospace.nasa.gov/programs_avsp.htm>.

[69] Institute of Medicine, 2000, *To Err Is Human: Building a Safer Health System*, National Academy Press, Washington, D.C. Available online at <http://books.nap.edu/catalog.php?record_id=9728>.

of medication errors by eliminating transcription errors. Although media attention tends to focus on the more exciting and exotic applications of software, a wider and deeper deployment of existing IT could have a profound effect on health care.[70] Computerization alone, however, is not sufficient; a highly dependable system with adequate levels of decision support is needed.[71]

The ability of software to implement complex functionality that cannot be implemented at reasonable cost in hardware makes new kinds of medical devices possible, such as heart and brain implants and new surgical tools and procedures. An exciting example of the potential of software to improve medical treatment is image-guided surgery, in which images produced by less recent technologies such as MRI can be synchronized with positioning data, allowing surgeons to see not only the physical surfaces of the area of surgery but also the internal structure revealed by prior imaging. A neurosurgeon removing a tumor aims to remove as much tumor material as possible without causing neurological damage; better tools allow less conservative but safer surgery. Obviously, the software supporting such a tool is critical and must be extraordinarily dependable.

OBSERVATIONS

This study raised a host of questions that have been asked many times before in the software engineering community and beyond but have still to be satisfactorily answered. How dependable is software today? Is dependability getting better or worse? How many accidents can be attributed to software failures? Which development methods are most cost-effective in delivering dependable software? Not surprisingly, this report does not answer these questions in full; answering any one of them comprehensively would require major research. Nevertheless, in the course of investigating the current state of software development and formulating its approach, the committee made some observations that inform its recommendations and reflect on these questions.

---

[70]Edward H. Shortliffe, 2005, "Strategic action in health information technology: Why the obvious has taken so long," *Health Affairs* 24(5):1222-1233.

[71]In one study of a hospital in Utah, 52 percent of admitted patients suffered from adverse drug events (ADEs), of which 9 percent resulted in serious harm, despite the use of a CPOE system intended to prevent them (Jonathan R. Nebeker, Jennifer M. Hoffman, Charlene R. Weir, Charles L. Bennett, and John F. Hurdle, 2005, "High rates of adverse drug events in a highly computerized hospital," *Archives of Internal Medicine* 165:1111-1116).

Observation 1: Lack of Evidence

Studies of this sort do not have the resources to perform their own data collection, so they rely instead on data collected, analyzed, and interpreted by others. Early on in this study, it became clear that very little information was available for addressing the most fundamental questions about software dependability.

Incomplete and unreliable data about software failures and about the efficacy of different approaches to the development of software make objective scientific evaluation difficult if not impossible. When software fails, the failures leave no evidence of fractured spars or metal fatigue to guide accident investigators; execution of software rarely causes changes to the software itself. Investigating the role of software in an accident needs a full understanding of the software design documents, the implementation, and the logs of system events recorded during execution, yet this expertise may be available only to the manufacturer, which may have a conflict of interest.

Failures in a complex system often involve fault propagation and complex interactions between hardware components, software components, and human operators. This makes it very difficult to precisely determine the impact of software on a system failure. Complex interactions and tight coupling not only make a system less reliable but also make its failures harder to diagnose. There are a number of compendia of anecdotal failure reports, most notably those collected by the Risks Forum,[72] which for many years has been gathering into a single archive a wide variety of reports of software-related problems, mostly from the popular press. The accident databases maintained by federal agencies (for example, the National Transportation Safety Board) include incidents in which software was implicated. But detailed analyses of software failures are few and far between, and those that have been made public are mostly the work of academics and researchers who based their analyses on secondary sources.

The lack of systematic reporting of significant software failures is a serious problem that hinders evaluation of the risks and costs of software failure and measurement of the effectiveness of new policies or interventions. In traditional engineering disciplines, the value of learning from failure is well understood,[73] and one could argue that without this feedback loop, software engineering cannot properly claim to be an engineer-

---

[72]See The Risks Digest, a forum on risks to the public in computers and related systems moderated by Peter G. Neumann. Available online at <http://catless.ncl.ac.uk/risks>.

[73]See, for example, Henry Petroski, 2004, *To Engineer Is Human*, St. Martin's Press, New York; and Matthys Levy and Mario Salvadori, 1992, *Why Buildings Fall Down*, W.W. Norton & Company, New York.

ing discipline at all. Of course, many companies track failures in their own software, but there is little attention paid by the field as a whole to historic failures and what can be learned from them.

This lack of evidence leads to a range of views within the broader community. The essential question is, If mechanisms for certifying software cannot be relied on, should the software be used or not? Some believe that absent evidence for dependability and robust certification mechanisms, a great deal of caution—even resistance—is warranted in deploying and using software-based systems, since there are risks that systems will be built that could have a catastrophic effect. Others observe that systems are being built, that software is being deployed widely, and that deployment of robust systems could in fact save lives, and they argue that the risk of a catastrophic event is worth taking. From this perspective, effects should focus not so much on deciding what to build, but rather on providing the guidance that is urgently needed by practitioners and users of systems. Accordingly, the lack of evidence has two direct consequences for this report. First, it has informed the key notions that evidence be at the core of dependable software development, that data collection efforts are needed, and that transparency and openness be encouraged so that those deploying software in critical applications are aware of the limits of evidence for its dependability and can make fully informed decisions about whether the benefits of deployment outweigh the residual risks. Second, it has tempered the committee's desire to provide prescriptive guidance—that is, the approach recommended by the committee is largely free of endorsements or criticisms of particular development approaches, tools, or techniques. Moreover, the report leaves to the developers and procurers of individual systems the question of what level of dependability is appropriate, and what costs are worth incurring in order to obtain it.

Observation 2: Not Just Bugs

Software, according to a popular view, fails because of bugs: errors in the code that cause the software to fail to meet its specification. In fact, only a tiny proportion of failures due to the mistakes of software developers can be attributed to bugs—3 percent in one study that focused on fatal accidents.[74] As is well known to software engineers (but not to the general public), by far the largest class of problems arises from errors made in the eliciting, recording, and analysis of requirements. A second large class of problems arises from poor human factors design. The two classes are

---

[74]Donald MacKenzie, 2001, *Mechanizing Proof: Computing, Risk, and Trust*, MIT Press, Cambridge, Mass., Chapter 9.

related; bad user interfaces usually reflect an inadequate understanding of the user's domain and the absence of a coherent and well-articulated conceptual model.

Security vulnerabilities are to some extent an exception; the overwhelming majority of security vulnerabilities reported in software products—and exploited to attack the users of such products—are at the implementation level. The prevalence of code-related problems, however, is a direct consequence of higher-level decisions to use programming languages, design methods, and libraries that admit these problems. In principle, it is relatively easy to prevent implementation-level attacks but hard to retrofit existing programs.

One insidious consequence of the focus on coding errors is that developers may be absolved from blame for other kinds of errors. In particular, inadequate specifications, misconceptions about requirements, and serious usability flaws are often overlooked, and users are unfairly blamed. The therapists who operated the radiotherapy system that failed in Panama, for example, were blamed for entering data incorrectly, even though the system had an egregious design flaw that permitted the entry of invalid data without generating a warning, and they were later tried in court for criminal negligence.[75] In several avionics incidents, pilots were blamed for issuing incorrect commands, even though researchers recognized that the systems themselves were to blame for creating "mode confusion."[76]

Understanding software failures demands a systems perspective, in which the software is viewed as one component of many, working in concert with other components—be they physical devices, human operators, or other computer systems—to achieve the desired effect. Such a perspective underlies the approach recommended in Chapter 3.

Observation 3: The Cost of Strong Approaches

In the last 20 years, new techniques have become available in which software can be specified and designed using precise notations and subsequently subjected to mechanized analysis. These techniques, often referred to as "formal methods," are believed by many to incur unreasonable costs. While it may be true that formal methods are not economical when only the lowest levels of dependability are required, there is some evidence that as dependability demands increase, an approach that includes formal specification and analysis becomes the more cost-effective

---

[75]See Deborah Gage and John McCormick, 2004, "We did nothing wrong," *Baseline*, March 4. Available online at <http://www.baselinemag.com/article2/0,1540,1543571,00.asp>.
[76]See NASA, 2001, "FM program: Analysis of mode confusion." Available online at <http://shemesh.larc.nasa.gov/fm/fm-now-mode-confusion.html>.

option. This section presents some data in support of this claim and gives a simple economic analysis showing how the choice between a traditional approach and a strong approach (one that incorporates formal methods) might be made.

Traditional software development approaches use specification and design notations that do not support rigorous analysis, as well as programming languages that are not fully defined or that defeat automated analysis. Traditional approaches depend on human inspection and testing for validation and verification. Strong approaches also use testing but employ notations and languages that are amenable to rigorous analysis, and they exploit mechanical tools for reasoning about properties of requirements, specifications, designs, and code.

Traditional approaches are generally less costly than strong methods for obtaining low levels of dependability, and for this reason many practitioners believe that strong methods are not cost-effective. The costs of traditional approaches, however, can increase exponentially with increasing levels of dependability. The cost of strong approaches increases more slowly with increasing dependability, meaning that at some level of dependability strong methods can be more cost-effective.[77]

Whether software firms and developers will use traditional or strong approaches depends, in part, on consumer demand for dependability. The following exercise discusses the consumer-demand-dependent conditions under which firms and developers would choose either the traditional or the strong approach and the conditions under which it would be sensible, from an economics and engineering perspective, to switch back to the traditional approach.

---

[77]Peter Amey, 2002, "Correctness by construction: Better can also be cheaper," *CrossTalk Magazine, The Journal of Defence Software Engineering*, March. Available online at <http://www.praxis-his.com/pdfs/c_by_c_better_cheaper.pdf>. This paper describes the savings that are repeatedly made by projects that use strong software engineering methods. On p. 27, Amey asks

> How . . . did SPARK help Lockheed reduce its formal FAA test costs by 80 percent? The savings arose from avoiding testing repetition by eliminating most errors before testing even began. . . . Most high-integrity and safety-critical developments make use of language subsets. Unfortunately, these subsets are usually informally designed and consist, in practice, of simply leaving out parts of the language thought to be likely to cause problems. Although this shortens the length of rope with which the programmers may hang themselves, it does not bring about any qualitative shift in what is possible. The use of coherent subsets free from ambiguities and insecurities does bring such a shift. Crucially it allows analysis to be performed on source code before the expensive test phase is entered. This analysis is both more effective and cheaper than manual methods such as inspections. Inspections should still take place but can focus on more profitable things like "does this code meet its specification" rather than "is there a possible data-flow error." Eliminating all these "noise" errors at the engineer's terminal greatly improves the efficiency of the test process because the testing can focus on showing that requirements have been met rather than becoming a "bug hunt."

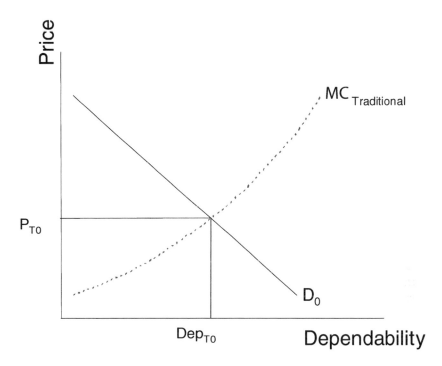

FIGURE 1.1 Equilibrium price and dependability with perfect competition and traditional software approaches.

Consumers have some willingness to pay for dependability. Like any other good, the more costly dependability is, the less of it consumers, who have limited resources, will purchase. Figure 1.1 shows this downward-sloping demand (D_0) for dependability: At low prices for dependability, consumers will purchase a lot of it; at high prices, they will purchase less. It is costly, meanwhile, for suppliers to increase dependability. The marginal cost of supplying different levels of dependability using traditional approaches is depicted by the line labeled "$MC_{Traditional}$." With perfect competition, the market will reach an equilibrium in which firms supply dependability, Dep_{T0}, at the price P_{T0}.

Next, consider the introduction of strong software engineering approaches (Figure 1.2). Consumers still have the same willingness to pay for dependability, but the costs of supplying any given amount of it now depend on whether the firm uses traditional approaches or strong engineering approaches, with the cost structure of the latter depicted in the figure by the curve labeled "MC_{Strong}."

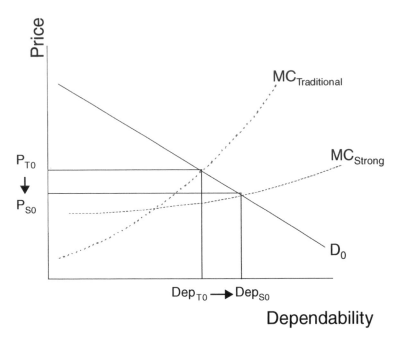

FIGURE 1.2 Lower equilibrium price and higher dependability with strong engineering approaches.

Consumers have the same demand profile for dependability as they had before, but the curve intersects the strong software cost profile at a different point, yielding a new equilibrium at higher dependability (Dep_{S0}) and lower price (P_{S0}).[78] It is a new equilibrium because, in a perfectly competitive market, firms that continue to use traditional approaches would be driven out of business by firms using strong approaches.

Lower prices and higher dependability are not necessarily the new equilibrium point. The new equilibrium depends crucially on the slopes and location of the demand and cost curves. For some goods, consumers might not be willing to pay as much for a given level of dependability as they might for other goods. Figure 1.3 depicts this demand profile as D_1. In this scenario, firms will continue to use traditional approaches, with the equilibrium Dep_{T1} at a price of P_{T1}. No rational firm would switch to strong approaches if consumer demand did not justify doing so.

---

[78]It is assumed here that the costs of switching to the new programming methods are incorporated into the MC_{Strong} curve.

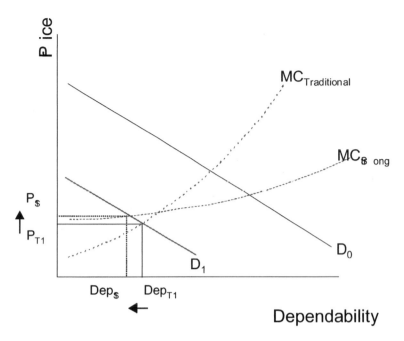

FIGURE 1.3 Consumer demand for dependability is decreased; there is no switch to strong approaches in equilibrium.

Observation 4: Coupling and Complexity

In *Normal Accidents*,[79] Perrow outlines two characteristics of systems that induce failures: interactive complexity, where components may interact in unanticipated ways, perhaps because of failures or just because no designer anticipated the interactions that could occur; and tight coupling, wherein a failure cannot be isolated but brings about other failures that cascade through the system. Systems heavy with software tend to have both attributes. The software may operate as designed, and the component it interfaces with may be performing within specifications, but the software design did not anticipate unusual, but still permissible, values in the component. (In one incident, avionics software sensed the pilot was performing a touch-and-go maneuver; this was because the wet tarmac did not allow the wheels to turn, so they skidded. The pilot was trying to land but the control assumed otherwise and would not let him deceler-

[79]Charles Perrow, 1999, *Normal Accidents*, Princeton University Press, Princeton, N.J.

ate.[80]) Or, the component may be used in a way not anticipated by the software specifications, or a newer model of the component is introduced without realizing how the software might affect it. (Both were true in the case in the Ariane 5 rocket failure. It was destroyed by the overflow of a horizontal velocity variable in a reused Ariane 4 component that was to perform a function not even required by Ariane 5.[81]) Complicated software programs interact with other complicated software programs, so many unexpected interactions can occur. Trying to find a single point of failure is often fruitless.

The interactive character of software and the components it interfaces with is, quite literally, tightly coupled, so faulty interactions can easily disturb the components linked to it, cascading the disturbance. Modularity reduces this tendency and reduces complexity. Redundant paths increase reliability; while they increase the number of components and the amount of software, this does not necessarily increase the interactive complexity and certainly not the coupling.

The problem of coupling and complexity is exacerbated by the drive for efficiency that underlies modern management techniques. It is common to use software systems in an attempt to increase an organization's efficiency by eliminating redundancy and shaving margins. In such circumstances, systems can tend to be drawn inexorably toward the dangerous combination of high complexity and high coupling. Cook and Rasmussen explain this phenomenon and illustrate its dangers in the context of patient care.[82] In one incident they describe, for example, a hospital allowed surgeries to begin on patients expected to need intensive care afterwards on the assumption that space in the intensive care unit would become available; when it did not, the surgery had to be terminated abruptly. In another incident, when a computer upgrade was introduced, the automated drug delivery program of a large hospital was disrupted for more than 2 days, neccesitating the manual rewriting of drug orders for all patients. All backup tapes of medication orders were corrupted "because of a complex interlocking process related to the database management software that was used by the pharmacy application. Under particular circumstances, tape backups could be incomplete in ways that

---

[80]See Main Commission Accident Investigation—Poland, 1994, "Report on the accident to Airbus A320-211 aircraft in Warsaw on 14 September 1993." Available online at <http://sunnyday.mit.edu/accidents/warsaw-report.html>.

[81]See J.L. Lions, 1996, "ARIANE 5: Flight 501 failure," Report by the Inquiry Board. Available online at <http://www.ima.umn.edu/~arnold/disasters/ariane5rep.html>.

[82]R. Cook and J. Rasmussen, 2005, "Going solid: A model of system dynamics and consequences for patient safety," Quality and Safety in Health Care 14(2):130-134.

remained hidden from the operator."[83] There was no harm to patients, but the disruption and effort required to mitigate it were enormous.

It is also well known that the operator interfaces to complex software systems are often so poorly designed that they invite operator error.[84] However, there is a more insidious danger that derives from a lack of confidence in systems assurance—namely, systems that might best be largely autonomous are instead dubbed "advisory" and placed under human supervision. For a human to monitor an automated system, the automation must generally expose elements of its internal state and operation; these are seldom designed to support an effective mental model, so the human may be left out of the loop and unable to perform effectively.[85] Such problems occur frequently in systems that operate in different modes, where the operator has to understand which mode the system is in to know its properties. Mode confusion contributing to an error is exemplified by the fatal crashes of two Airbus 320s—one in Warsaw in 1993 and one near Bangalore in 1990.[86] Systems thinking invites consideration of such combinations (sometimes called "mixed initiative systems") in which the operator is viewed as a component and the overall system design takes adequate account of human cognitive functions.

These concerns do not necessarily militate against the use of software, but they do suggest that careful attention should be paid to the risks of interactive complexity and tight coupling and the advantages of modularity, buffering, and redundancy; that interdependences among components of critical software systems should be analyzed to ensure that modes of

---

[83]Richard Cook and Michael O'Connor, forthcoming, "Thinking about accidents and systems," in *Improving Medication Safety*, K. Thompson and H. Manasse, eds., American Society of Health-System Pharmacists, Washington, D.C.

[84]See, for example, Ross Koppel, Joshua P. Metlay, Abigail Cohen, Brian Abaluck, A. Russell Localio, Stephen E. Kimmel, and Brian L. Strom, 2005, "Role of computerized physician order entry systems in facilitating medication errors," *Journal of the American Medical Association* 293(10):1197-1203.

[85]One comprehensive study of this phenomenon is P.J. Smith, E. McCoy, and C. Layton, 1997, "Brittleness in the design of cooperative problem-solving systems: The effects on user performance," *IEEE Transactions on Systems, Man and Cybernetics* 27:360-371. See also C. Layton, P.J. Smith, and C.E. McCoy, 1994, "Design of a cooperative problem-solving system for en-route flight planning: An empirical evaluation," *Human Factors* 36:94-119. For an overview of this and related work see D.D. Woods and E. Hollnagel, 2006, *Joint Cognitive Systems: Patterns in Cognitive Systems Engineering*, Taylor & Francis, Boca Raton, Fla.

[86]The report in *Flight International* (May 2-8, 1990) on the Bangalore crash makes very interesting reading. The account of the number of flight modes which the A320 went through in the 2 minutes before the crash and the side effects of each (which seem not to have been understood properly by the pilots) makes operating an A320 appear very different from flying a fully manual airplane. The secondary effects (such as selecting a target altitude that causes the engines to be retarded to idle, and needing several seconds to develop full power again) need to be well understood by the pilots.

failure are well understood; and that failures are localized to the greatest extent possible. Developers and procurers of software systems should also keep in mind that there are likely to be trade-offs of various sorts between the goals of efficiency and safety and that achieving appropriate safety margins may exact a cost in reduced efficiency and perhaps also in reduced functionality and automation. At the same time, the clarification and simplification that meeting most safety requirements demands may also improve efficiency. Recent work on engineering resilience suggests ways to dynamically manage the trade-off and ways to think about when to sacrifice efficiency for safety.[87]

Observation 5: Safety Culture Matters

The efficacy of a certification regimen or development process does not necessarily result directly from the technical properties of its constituent practices. The de facto avionics standard, DO178B, for example, although it contains much good advice, imposes (as explained above) some elaborate procedures that may not have a direct beneficial effect on dependability. And yet avionics software has an excellent record with remarkably few failures, which many in the field credit to the adoption of DO178B.

One possible explanation is that the strictures of the standard and the domain in which system engineers and developers are working have collateral effects on the larger cultural framework in which software is developed beyond their immediate technical effects. The developers of avionics software are confronted with the fact that many lives depend directly on the software they are constructing and they pay meticulous attention to detail. A culture tends to evolve that leads developers to act cautiously, to not rely on intuition, and to value the critiques of others.

Richard Feynman, in his analysis of the Challenger disaster,[88] commented on similar attitudes among software engineers at NASA:

> The software is checked very carefully in a bottom-up fashion. . . . But completely independently there is an independent verification group, that takes an adversary attitude to the software development group, and

---

[87]See, for example, D.D. Woods, 2006, "Essential characteristics of resilience for organizations," in *Resilience Engineering: Concepts and Precepts*, E. Hollnagel, D.D. Woods, and N. Leveson, eds., Ashgate, Aldershot, United Kingdom; D.D. Woods, 2005, "Creating foresight: Lessons for resilience from Columbia," in *Organization at the Limit: NASA and the Columbia Disaster*, W.H. Starbuck and M. Farjoun, eds., Blackwell, Malden, Mass.

[88]Richard P. Feynman, 1986, "Appendix F—Personal observations on the reliability of the shuttle," In *Report of the Presidential Commission on the Space Shuttle Challenger Accident*, June. Available online at <http://science.ksc.nasa.gov/shuttle/missions/51-l/docs/rogers-commission/Appendix-F.txt>.

tests and verifies the software as if it were a customer of the delivered product. . . . A discovery of an error during verification testing is considered very serious, and its origin studied very carefully to avoid such mistakes in the future.

To summarize then, the computer software checking system and attitude is of the highest quality. There appears to be no process of gradually fooling oneself while degrading standards so characteristic of the Solid Rocket Booster or Space Shuttle Main Engine safety systems.

An organizational culture that encourages and supports such attitudes is called a "safety culture," and it is widely recognized as an essential ingredient in the engineering of critical systems. At the same time, it is important to recognize that a strong safety culture, while necessary, is not sufficient. As Feynman noted in the same analysis: "One might add that the elaborate system could be very much improved by more modern hardware and programming techniques." A safety culture and the processes that support it need to be accompanied by the best technical practices in order to achieve desired dependability.[89]

Establishing a good safety culture is not an easy matter and requires a sustained effort. The task is easier in the context of organizations that already have strong safety cultures in their engineering divisions and in industries that have organizational commitments to safety (and pressure from consumers to deliver safe products).[90] The airline industry is a good example. The large companies that produce avionics software have a long history of engineering large-scale critical systems. There is a rich assemblage of organizations and institutions with an interest in safety; accidents are vigorously investigated; standards are strict; liabilities established; and its customers are influential and resourceful. In his book on accident

---

[89]The safety culture alone may prevent the deployment of dangerous systems, but it may exact an unreasonably high cost. NASA's avionics software for the space shuttle, for example, is estimated to have cost roughly $1,000 per line of code (Dennis Jenkins, "Advanced vehicle automation and computers aboard the shuttle." Available online at <http://history.nasa.gov/sts25th/pages/computer.html>, updated April 5, 2001). Using appropriate tools and techniques can help reduce cost (see previous discussion of the cost of strong approaches). Studies of some systems developed by Praxis, for example, show that software was obtained with defect rates comparable to the software produced by the most exacting standards, but at costs not significantly higher than for conventional developments (Anthony Hall, 1996, "Using formal methods to develop an ATC information system," *IEEE Software* 13(2):66-76). It is not clear how widely these results could be replicated, but it is clear that conventional methods based on testing and manual review become prohibitively expensive when very high dependability is required.

[90]For a comprehensive discussion of the role of safety culture in a variety of industries, see Charles Perrow, 1999, *Normal Accidents*, Princeton University Press, Princeton, N.J.

investigation,[91] Chris Johnson lists a dozen public and nonprofit organizations concerned with software reliability in the industry (and notes the lack of incident reporting even there). A strong safety culture has not been as widespread in some other domains.

Standards and certification regimes can play a major role in establishing and strengthening safety cultures within companies. The processes they mandate contribute directly to the safety culture, but there are important indirect influences also. They raise the standards of professionalism, the abilities they demand leads to the weeding out of less-skilled engineers, and they call for a seriousness of purpose (and a willingness to perform some laborious work whose benefit may not be immediately apparent). The need to conform to a standard or obtain certification imposes unavoidable costs on a development organization. One engineer interviewed by the committee explained that in his department (in a large U.S. computer company), the fact that managers were forced to spend money on safety made them more open and willing to consider better practices in general and somewhat counterbalanced the tendency to focus on expanding the feature set of a product and hurrying the product to market.

---

[91]C.W. Johnson, 2003, *Failure in Safety-Critical Systems: A Handbook of Accident and Incident Reporting*, University of Glasgow Press, Glasgow, Scotland. Available online at <http://www.dcs.gla.ac.uk/~johnson/book/>.

2

Proposed Approach

T his chapter is the core of the report. It describes an approach to the development of dependable software that the committee believes could be widely adopted, and would be more effective than the approaches that are currently in widespread use.

The proposed approach can be summarized in three key points—"the three *Es*":

- *Explicit claims.* No system can be dependable in all respects and under all conditions. So to be useful, a claim of dependability must be explicit. It must articulate precisely the properties the system is expected to exhibit and the assumptions about the system's environment on which the claim is contingent. The claim should also make explicit the level of dependability claimed, preferably in quantitative terms. Different properties may be assured to different levels of dependability.
- *Evidence.* For a system to be regarded as dependable, concrete evidence must be present that substantiates the dependability claim. This evidence will take the form of a "dependability case," arguing that the required properties follow from the combination of the properties of the system itself (that is, the implementation) and the environmental assumptions. So that independent parties can evaluate it, the dependability case must be perspicuous and well-structured; as a rule of thumb, the cost of reviewing the case should be at least an order of magnitude less than the cost of constructing it. Because testing alone is usually insufficient to establish properties, the case will typically combine evidence from testing

with evidence from analysis. In addition, the case will inevitably involve appeals to the process by which the software was developed—for example, to argue that the software deployed in the field is the same software that was subjected to analysis or testing.

• *Expertise.* Expertise—in software development, in the domain under consideration, and in the broader systems context, among other things—is necessary to achieve dependable systems. Flexibility is an important advantage of the proposed approach; in particular the developer is not required to follow any particular process or use any particular method or technology. This flexibility provides experts the freedom to employ new techniques and to tailor the approach to their application and domain. However, the requirement to produce evidence is extremely demanding and likely to stretch today's best practices to their limit. It will therefore be essential that the developers are familiar with best practices and diverge from them only with good reason. Expertise and skill will be needed to effectively utilize the flexibility the approach provides and discern which best practices are appropriate for the system under consideration and how to apply them. This chapter contains a short catalog of best practices, judged by the committee to be those that are most important for dependability.

These notions—to be explicit, to demand and produce evidence, and to marshall expertise—are, in one sense, entirely traditional and uncontroversial. Modern engineering of physical artifacts marshals evidence for product quality by measuring items against explicit criteria, and licensing is often required in an attempt to ensure expertise. Applying these notions to software, however, is not straightforward, and many of the assumptions that underlie statistical process control (which has governed the design of production lines since the 1920s) do not hold for software. Some of the ways in software systems differ from more traditional engineering projects include the following:

• *Criteria.* The criteria for physical artifacts are often simpler, often comprising no more than a failure or breakage rate for the artifact as a whole. Because of the complexity of software and its interdependence on the environment in which it operates, explicit and precise articulation of claims is both more challenging and more important than for traditional engineering.

• *Feasibility of testing.* For physical artifacts, limited testing provides compelling evidence of quality, with the continuity of physical phenomena allowing widespread inferences to be drawn from only a few sample points. In contrast, limited testing of software can rarely provide compelling evidence of behavior under all conditions.

• *Process/product correlation.* The fundamental premise of statistical quality control is that sampling the product coming out of a process gives a measure of the quality of the process itself, which in turn will determine the quality of items that are not sampled. Although better software process can lead to better software, the correlation is not sufficiently strong to provide evidence of dependability. Unlike physical engineering, in which large classes of identical artifacts are produced, software engineering rarely produces the same artifact twice, so evidence about one software system rarely bears on another such system. And even an organization with the very best process can produce seriously flawed software.

These differences have profound implications, so that the application of standard engineering principles to software results in an approach that is far from traditional. Practitioners are likely to find the proposed approach radical in three respects. First, the articulation of explicit dependability claims suggests that software systems requirements should be structured differently, with requirements being prioritized (separating the crucial dependability properties from other desirable, but less crucial, ones) and environmental assumptions being elevated to greater prominence. Second, the standard of evidence for a system that must meet a high level of dependability cannot generally be achieved using the kind of testing regimen that is accepted by many certification schemes today. Instead, it will be necessary to show an explicit connection between the tests performed and the properties claimed; the inevitable gap will likely have to be filled by analysis. Third, constructing the dependability case after the implementation is complete will not usually be feasible. Instead, considerations of the ease of constructing the case will permeate the development, influencing the choice of features, the architecture, the implementation language, and so on, and the need to preserve the chain of evidence will call for a rigorous process. Achieving all of this will demand significant and broad-ranging *expertise*.

Lest the reader be concerned that the proposed approach is too risky, it should be noted that although widespread adoption of the proposed approach would be a radical change for the software industry, the constituent practices that the approach would require are far from novel and have been used successfully in complex, critical software projects for over a decade. Moreover, the underlying sensibility of the approach is consistent with the attitude advocated by the field of systems engineering—often referred to as "systems thinking"—whose validity is widely accepted and repeatedly reaffirmed by accidents and failures that occur when it is not applied.

Because the proposed approach is very different from the approach used to build most software today, it will not only require a change in mindset but will also probably demand skills that are in short supply. A radical improvement in software will therefore depend on improvements in education (e.g., better curricula). Furthermore, the high standards imposed by this approach may not always be achievable at reasonable cost. In some cases, this will mean reducing expectations of dependability—in other words, limiting the functionality and complexity of the system. If no acceptable trade-off can be agreed upon, it may not be possible to build the system at all using today's technology. Without major advances brought about by fundamental research, many software systems that society will want or need in the coming decade will probably be impossible to build to appropriate dependability standards. The approach advocated here is technology-neutral, so as technology advances, more effective and economical means of achieving society's goals will become possible, and systems that cannot be built today may be feasible in the future.

EXPLICIT DEPENDABILITY CLAIMS

What Is Dependability?

Until now, this report has relied on the reader's informal understanding of the term "dependable." This section clarifies the way in which the term is used in the context of this report.

The list of adjectives describing the demands placed on software has grown steadily. Software must be reliable and available; usable and flexible; maintainable and adaptable; and so on. It would not be helpful simply to add "dependable" to this long list, with the meaning that a "dependable" software system is one on which the user can depend.

One could imagine, though, that demanding dependability in this broad sense from a software system is not unreasonable. After all, do not users of all kinds of nonsoftware systems demand, and obtain, dependability from them? Since the late 1970s, for example, drivers have come to expect all-round dependability from their cars. But large software systems are more complex than most other engineered systems, and while it might make sense to demand dependability from a car in its entirety, it makes less sense to demand the same of a large software system. It is clear what services are expected of a car: If the car fails in deep water, for example, few drivers would think to point to that as a lack of dependability.[1] Most

---

[1]Incidentally, the increasing complexity of automobile electronic systems means that accidental systems may form and the dependability problems experienced in complex software systems may appear in automobiles. A recent example was the discovery of a "sneak circuit": If the radio was switched on and the brake pedal was depressed at the same time as a rear window was being operated, the air bags deployed. Fortunately, this was detected by simulation tools examining the electronic design, and no vehicles had to be recalled. Reported by committee member Martyn Thomas.

large software systems, in contrast, perform a large range of complex functions in a complex and changing environment. Users are not typically aware of a system's inherent limitations, nor can they always even detect changes in the environment that might compromise the system's reliability.

For these reasons, the dependability of a software system cannot be judged by a simple metric. A system is dependable only with respect to particular claimed properties; unless these properties are made explicit, dependability has little meaning. Moreover, dependability is not a local property of software that can be determined module by module but has to be articulated and evaluated from a systems perspective that takes into account the context of usage. A system may be dependable even though some of its functions fail repeatedly; conversely, it may be regarded as undependable if it causes unexpected effects in its environment, even if it suffers no obvious failures. These issues are discussed in more detail below (see "Software as a System Component").

In addition, dependability does not reside solely within a system but is also reflected in the degree of trust that its users are willing to place in it. Systems may meet all of their dependability requirements, but if users cannot be convinced that this is so, the systems will not be seen as dependable. That is, dependability is an "ability to deliver service that can justifiably be trusted,"[2] and for such justification, evidence will be required.

Why Claims Must Be Explicit

With limitless resources, it might be possible to build a system that is highly dependable in all of its properties, but in practice—for systems of even minimal complexity—this will not be achievable at a reasonable cost. A key characteristic of a system designed with dependability in mind will therefore be differentiation—that is, the properties of the system will not be uniform in the confidence they warrant but, on the contrary, will be assured to (possibly dramatically) differing degrees of confidence.

It follows that the users of a system can depend on it only if they know which properties can be relied upon. In other words, the crucial properties should be explicitly articulated and made clear not only to the user, as consumer of the system, but also to the developer, as its producer. Currently, consumer software is typically sold with few explicit representations of the properties it offers or its fitness for any purpose. Apple and Adobe, for example, provide software "as is" and "with all faults" and

---

[2]A. Avizienis, J.C. Laprie, B. Randell, and C. Landwehr, 2004, "Basic concepts and taxonomy of dependable and secure computing," *IEEE Transactions on Dependable and Secure Computing* 1(1):11-33.

disclaim all warranties. Google offers "no warranties whatsoever" for its services, and Microsoft warrants only that the software will "perform substantially in accordance with the accompanying materials for a period of (ninety) 90 days."[3] Software systems that are developed specially for a particular client are typically built to meet preagreed requirements, but these requirements are often a long and undifferentiated list of detailed functions.

Software as a System Component

Engineering fields with long experience in building complex systems (for example, aerospace, chemicals, and nuclear engineering) have developed approaches based on systems thinking; these approaches focus on the properties of the system as a whole and on the interactions among its components, especially those (often neglected) between a component being constructed and the components of its environment.

Systems thinking can have impacts on component design that may surprise those who have not encountered such thinking before. For example, the designer of a component viewed in isolation may think it a good idea to provide graceful degradation in response to perceived error situations. In a systems context, however, this could have negative consequences: For example, another component might be better placed to respond to the error, but its response might be thwarted by the gracefully degraded behavior of the original component, and its own attempts to work around this degraded behavior could have further negative consequences elsewhere. It might have been better for the original component simply to have shut itself down in response to the error.

As software has come to be deployed in—indeed has enabled— increasingly complex systems, the systems aspects have come to dominate in questions of software dependability. Dependability is not an intrinsic property of software. Software is merely one component of a system and a software component may be dependable in the context of one system but not dependable in another.[4]

---

[3]See, for example, warranty and disclaimer information at the following Web pages for each of the companies mentioned: <http://www.adobe.com/products/eula/warranty/> (Adobe); <http://www.apple.com/legal/sla/macosx.html> (Apple); <http://www.microsoft.com/windowsxp/home/eula.mspx> (Microsoft); and <http://desktop.google.com/eula.html> (Google).

[4]The guidance software for the Ariane 4 rocket was dependable as part of that system, but when it was reused in the Ariane 5, the assumptions about its operating environment were no longer valid, and the system failed catastrophically. J.L. Lions, 1996, "ARIANE 5: Flight 501 failure," Report by the Inquiry Board. Available online at <http://www.cs.unibo.it/~laneve/papers/ariane5rep.html>.

A system is not simply the sum of its components: A system causes its components to interact in ways that can be positive (producing desirable emergent behavior) or negative (often leading to surprising outcomes, including failures). Consequently, the properties of a system may not be related in a simple way to those of its components: It is possible to have a faulty system composed of correct components, and it is possible for a system correctly to achieve certain properties despite egregious flaws in its components.

Generally, what systems components should do is spelled out in their requirements and specification documents. These documents assume, but sometimes do not articulate, a certain environment. When placed in a system context, however, some of these assumptions may be violated. That is, the actual operational profile includes circumstances for which there may be no specified behavior (which means it is unclear what will happen) or for which the specified behavior is actually inappropriate. When these circumstances are encountered, failure often results. These sources of system failure are far more common, and often far more serious, than those due to simple bugs or coding errors.

People—the operators, users (and even the developers and maintainers) of a system—may also be viewed as system components. If a system meets its dependability criteria only if people act in certain ways, then those people should be regarded as part of the system, and an estimate of the probability of them behaving as required should be part of the evidence for dependability.[5] For example, if airline pilots are assumed to behave in a certain way as part of the dependability claim for an aircraft, then their training and the probability of human error become part of the system dependability analysis.

Accidental Systems and Criticality Creep

Many enterprises introduce software, or software-enabled functions, into their organization without realizing that they are constructing a system or modifying an existing system. For example, a hospital may introduce a wireless network to allow physicians to access various databases from handheld PDAs and may link databases (for example, patient and pharmacy records) to better monitor for drug interactions. Those developing software to perform these integrations often encounter systems issues but may not recognize them as such. For example, they may recognize that network protocols introduce potential vulnerabilities and will consider the security of the wireless connection and the appropriate

---

[5] SW01, the European standard for ground-based air traffic control systems, incorporates this approach.

cryptography to employ, but they may not recognize the larger systems issues of linking previously separate systems with their own security and access control policies.

As another example, emergency care units may have a dozen or more different medical devices connected to the same patient. These devices are designed and developed in isolation, but they form an accidental system (that is, a system constructed without conscious intent) whose components interact through the patient's physiology and through the cognitive and organizational faculties of the attending physicians and nurses. Each device typically attempts to monitor and support the stabilization of some parameter (heart rate, breathing, blood chemistry) but it does so in ignorance of the others even though these parameters are physiologically coupled. The result can be suboptimal whole-body stabilization[6] and legitimate concern that faults in a device, or in its operation, may propagate to other devices. Because they are designed in isolation, the devices have separate operator interfaces and may present similar information in different ways and require similar operations to be performed in different ways, thereby inviting operator errors.

A consequence of accidental system construction is that components may come to be used in contexts for which they were not designed and in which properties (typically internal failures and response to external faults) that were benign in their original context become more serious. An example is the use of desktop software in mission critical systems, as in the case of U.S.S. Yorktown, whose propulsion system failed on September 21, 1997, due to a software failure. An engineer with the Atlantic Fleet Technical Support Center attributed the failure to the integration and configuration of a commodity operating system without providing for adequate separation and process isolation.[7]

A more subtle but pervasive form of criticality creep occurs when the distinction between safety-critical and mission-critical features becomes blurred as users become dependent on features that they previously lived without. An avionics system, for example, might provide a moving map display—generally not flight-critical—that produces information for a pilot, on which the pilot might come to depend.

The formation of accidental systems may not always be avoidable, but it can be mitigated in two ways. The developer may be able to limit

---

[6]See, for example, a talk given by Timothy Buchman titled "Devices, data, information, treatment: A bedside perspective from the intensive care unit" at the June 2005 High Confidence Medical Device Software and Systems Workshop in Philadelphia, Pennsylvania. More information can be found online at <http://rtg.cis.upenn.edu/hcmdss/index.php3>.

[7]See Gregory Slabodkin, 1998, "Software glitches leave Navy smart ship dead in the water," *Government Computer News*, July 13. Available online at <http://www.gcn.com/print/17_17/33727-1.html>.

the exposure of the system as a whole to failures in some components, by designing interfaces carefully. For example, if a medical device is to be integrated into a hospital-wide information system, the developer might erect firewalls in the design of the software and hardware to ensure that the critical functions of the device cannot be controlled remotely. If this is not possible, the accidental system effect can be countered by recognizing the scope of the system as a whole and ensuring that the dependability case covers it.

Evolution and Recertification

Because systems and their operating environments evolve, a system that was dependable at the time it was introduced may become undependable after some time, necessitating a review and perhaps reworking of its dependability case. This review may conclude that the system no longer meets its original dependability criteria in its new environment. If so, the system may need to be modified, replaced, withdrawn from service, or simply accepted as being undependable.

When a system has been accepted as fit to put into service and it has been in use for some time, two issues may arise. First (and most commonly) something will happen—perhaps a bug fix, or the modification of a feature, or a change to an interface—that requires that the software be changed. How should the modified system be recertified as fit for service? A modified system is a new system, and local changes may affect the behavior of unmodified parts of the system, through interactions with the modified code or even (in many programming languages) as a result of recompilation of unmodified code. The evidence for dependability should therefore be reexamined whenever the system is modified and, if the evidence is no longer compelling, new evidence of dependability should be generated and the dependability case amended to reflect the changes. Ideally, most of the dependability case will be reusable. It is also important to rerun the system test suite (including additional tests showing that any known faults have indeed been corrected) as software maintenance can subtly violate the assumptions on which the dependability case was originally based.

Second, in-service experience may show that the dependability case made incorrect assumptions about the environment. For example, a protection system for an industrial process may have the dependability requirement that it fails no more frequently than once in every thousand demands, based on an assumption that the control system would limit the calls on the protection system to no more than 10 each year. After a few months of service, it might be apparent that the protection system is being called far more often than was assumed would happen. In such cases, the system should be taken out of service (or protected in some other way that is known to have the necessary dependability) until the dependability case has been reexamined under the new assumptions and shown to be adequate, or until sufficient additional evidence of the dependability of the protection system has been obtained.

Third, in the security case, if a new class of vulnerability is discovered, software that was understood to be secure might become vulnerable. In such a case new tests, tools, or review processes must be developed and applied, and the system updated as needed to operate in the new threat environment. The level of revision required to make the system's security acceptable in the face of the new threat will vary depending on the scope and impact of the vulnerability.

What to Make Explicit

The considerations in the previous sections suggest two important principles regarding what should be made explicit. First, it makes no sense to talk about certifiable dependability and justifiable confidence without defining the elements of the service that must be delivered if the system is to be considered dependable. In general, this will be a subset of the complete service provided by the system: Some requirements will not be considered important with respect to dependability in the specific context under consideration. Nor will it always be necessary to guarantee conformance to these properties to the highest degree. Dependability is not necessarily something that must be applied to all aspects of a system, and a system that is certified as dependable need not work perfectly all the time. Second, any claim about a service offered by a software component will be contingent on assumptions about the environment, and these assumptions will need to be made explicit.

Stating the requirements for a particular software component will generally involve three steps:

• The first step is to be explicit about the desired properties: to articulate the functional dependability properties precisely. These should be requirements properties expressed in terms of the expected impact of the software in its environment rather than specification properties limited to the behavior of the software at its interface with other components of the larger system (see next section).

• The second step is to be explicit about the degree of dependence that will be placed on each property. This may be expressed as the probability of failure on demand (pfd) or per hour (pfh) or as a mean time between failures (MTBF). In general, the dependence on different properties will be different: For example, it might be tolerable for a rail signal to give an incorrect "stop" command once every 10,000 hours but an incorrect "go" would be tolerated only once every 100 million hours, because the former would only cause delay, whereas the latter might cause a fatal accident.

- The third step is to be explicit about the environmental assumptions. These assumptions will generally include a characterization of the system or systems within which the software should be dependable and particular assumed properties of those systems. These properties may be arbitrarily complex, but sometimes they may involve little more than ranges of conditions under which the system will be operating. For example, an airborne collision-avoidance system may dependably provide separation for all geometries of two conflicting aircraft approaching each other at less than Mach 1 but become undependable if the approach is at Mach 2 (because the alerts could not be given in time for effective action to be taken) or when more than two aircraft are in conflict (because resolving the conflict between two aircraft might endanger the third).

Requirements, Specifications, and Domain Assumptions

The properties of interest to the user of a system are typically located in the physical world: that a radiotherapy machine deliver a certain dose, that a telephone transmit a sound wave faithfully, that a printer make appropriate ink marks on paper, and so on. The software, on the other hand, is typically specified in terms of properties at its interfaces, which usually involve phenomena that are not of direct interest to the user: that the radiotherapy machine, telephone, or printer send or receive certain signals at certain ports, with the inputs related to the outputs according to some rules.

It is important, therefore, to distinguish the requirements of a software system, which involve properties in the physical world, from the specification of a software system, which characterizes the behavior of the software system at its interface with the environment.[8] When the software system is itself only one component of a larger system, the other components in the system (including perhaps, as explained above, the people who work with the system) will be viewed as part of the environment.

One fundamental aspect of a systems perspective, as outlined in the early sections of this chapter, is paying attention to this distinction. Indeed, many failures of software systems can be attributed exactly to a

---

[8]These definitions of the terms "requirements" and "specification" come from Michael Jackson (see footnote 11 below) and are not conventional. In standard usage, the distinction between the two is rather vague, with requirements being used for descriptions that are produced earlier in a development with more involvement of the customer.

failure to recognize this distinction, in which undue emphasis was placed on the specification at the expense of the requirements. The properties that matter to the users of a system are the requirements; the properties the software developer can enforce are represented by the specification; and the gap between the two should be filled by properties of the environment itself.

The dependability properties of a software system, therefore, should be expressed as requirements, and the dependability case should demonstrate how these properties follow from the combination of the specification and the environmental assumptions.

In some cases, the requirements, specification, and environmental and domain assumptions will talk about the same set of phenomena. More often, though, the phenomena that can be directly controlled or monitored by the software system are not the same phenomena of interest to the user. A key step, therefore, in articulating the dependability properties, is to identify these sets of phenomena and classify them according to whether they lie at the interface or beyond. In large systems involving multiple components, it will be profitable to consider all the various interfaces between the components and to determine which phenomena are involved at each interface.

This viewpoint is illustrated in Figure 2.1. The outermost box represents the collection of phenomena in the world that are relevant to the problem the software is designed to address. The box labeled "machine" represents the phenomena of the software system being built (and the machine it runs on). The box labeled "environment" represents the phenomena of the components in the environment in which the software operates, including other computer systems, physical devices, and the human operators about whom assumptions are made. The box labeled "user" represents the phenomena involving the users. The gray borders of the boxes represent shared phenomena. The three spots denote archetypal phenomena. The phenomenon m is internal to the machine and invisible from outside; the instructions that execute inside the computer, for example, are such phenomena. The phenomenon s is a specification phenomenon, at the interface of the machine, shared with its environment. The phenomenon r is a requirements phenomenon, visible to the user and shared with the environment but not with the machine. This view simplifies the situation somewhat. It also shows the user as distinct from the environment, in order to emphasize that the phenomena that the user experiences (labeled r) are not generally the same as the phenomena controlled by the software (labeled s). In practice, the sets of specification and requirement phenomena overlap, and the user cannot be cleanly separated from the environment.

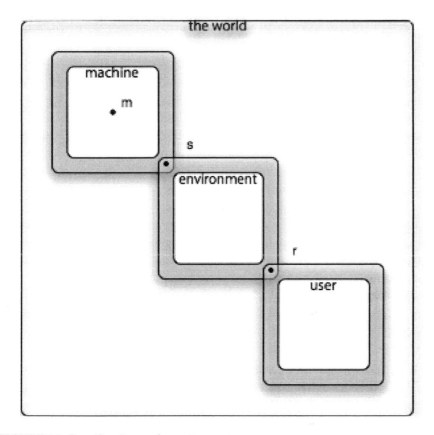

FIGURE 2.1 Specification and requirements.

The dependability case will involve *m*, *s*, and *r*. The argument will have two pieces. First, a correctness argument for the software will show how *s* follows from *m*: that is, how the intended properties of the software system at its interface are ensured by its implementation. Second, a specification-requirements argument will show how *r* follows from *s*: that is, how the desired requirement as observed by the user is ensured by the behavior of the software system at its interface. The correctness argument can be constructed in terms of the software alone and is entirely formal (in the sense that it does not involve any notions that cannot in principle be perfectly formalized). The specification-requirements argument, on the other hand, must combine knowledge about the software system with knowledge of the environment. In its general form, it will say that the requirements follow from the combination of the specification and the properties of the environment. This argument cannot usually be entirely formal, because determining the properties of the environment will in general have to be an informal matter. So whereas the correctness argument is in theory amenable to mechanized checking, the specification-requirements argument will rest on assumptions about the environment that will need to be confirmed by domain experts. To illustrate the idea, here are some examples:

- *Traffic lights.* The key dependability property of a traffic light system at a particular intersection is to prevent accidents. This is a requirement, and the phenomenon of two cars crashing is an example of an *r*. The software system interacts with the environment by receiving sensor inputs and generating control signals for the lights; these are the *s* phenomena. Assumptions about the environment include that the sensor and traffic light units satisfy certain specifications (for example, that a control signal sent to a traffic light will change the light in a certain way) and that the drivers behave in certain ways (for example, stopping at red lights and not in the middle of the intersection).

- *Radiotherapy.* A key dependability property of a radiotherapy system is to not deliver an overdose to the patient. The phenomena *r* are those involving the location of the target of the beam, the dosage delivered, the identity of the patient, and so on. The software system interacts with the operator through user interfaces and with the physical devices that control and monitor the beam settings. Assumptions include that the physical devices behave in certain ways and obey commands issued to them within certain tolerances, that the patient behaves in a certain way (not moving during irradiation, for example), and that the human organization of the facility obeys certain rules (such as preventing other people from entering the treatment room when the beam is on and ensuring that the correct patient is placed on the bed).

- *Criminal records.* A dependability property of a system for maintaining criminal records may be that no records are permanently lost. The phenomena *r* involve the records and the means by which they are created and accessed. The phenomena *s* at the interface of the software system might include these and, in addition, commands sent to a disk drive. The key assumptions, for example, are that the disk drive offers certain reliability guarantees and that unauthorized access to the file system is prevented. The demarcation between a software system and its environment is not always clear and will often be determined as much by economic and organizational issues as by technical ones. For example, if the criminal records system is built on top of an existing service (such as a database or replicated file system), that service will be regarded as part of the environment.

The Warsaw airport Airbus accident in September 1993 has been cited as an example of a failure to distinguish between specifications and requirements. An Airbus A320-211 came in to land in heavy winds. The aircraft aquaplaned for 9 seconds before reverse thrust was enabled, overran the runway, and collided with an embankment, killing 1 pilot and seriously injuring 2 other crew members and 51 passengers. The reverse thrust system was designed to be disabled under software control unless both left and the right landing gears were under compression, indicating contact with the ground. The software met its specification flawlessly, but unfortunately the specification did not match the desired dependability property. The crucial property, a requirement, was that reverse thrust should be disabled only when airborne, and this was certainly not satisfied. Had the dependability of the system been expressed and evaluated in terms of this property, attention might have been drawn to the domain assumption that lack of compression always accompanies being airborne, and the construction of a dependability case might have revealed that this assumption was invalid.[9]

The inevitable gap between specification and requirements properties speaks directly to the dependability of a service provision. At a minimum, software developers must appreciate this distinction, and as part of developing a dependable case there should be accountability for ensuring that the specification properties guarantee the requirements properties and for providing evidence (in the form of justifiable environmental assumptions) for this connection. A useful analogy may be the role of architects in the design of a new building: The architects capture the extrinsic requirements (accommodation needs, relationships between different rooms, workflow, aesthetic considerations); they add the safety requirements and regulatory requirements and, with the help of specialists such as structural engineers, convert the whole into a set of specifications that can be implemented by a construction firm. The architects accept responsibility and accountability for the relationship between extrinsic and intrinsic requirements.

The idea of distinguishing requirements from specifications is not new. In process control, the need to express requirements in terms of observable, extrinsic properties has long been recognized and was codified

---

[9]The official report of this incident has been translated by Peter Ladkin and can be found online (see below). Interestingly, although the report notes in its recommendations the deficiencies of the software, it attributes the cause of the accident to the flight crew, blaming them for not aborting the landing. See Peter Ladkin, transcriber, 1994, "Transcription of report on the accident to Airbus A320-211 aircraft in Warsaw on 14 September 1993," Main Commission, Aircraft Accident Investigation, Warsaw. Available online at <http://www.rvs.uni-bielefeld.de/publications/Incidents/DOCS/ComAndRep/Warsaw/warsaw-report.html>.

in Parnas's four-variable model.[10] It distinguishes the specification phenomena—the inputs and outputs of the machine—from the requirements phenomena—the monitored and controlled variables—thus accounting for the imperfections of the monitors and actuators that mediate between the machine and the environment. Recent work has extended this to systems of more general structure.[11]

EVIDENCE

A user should not depend on a system without some evidence that confidence is justified. Dependability and evidence of dependability are thus inseparable, and a system whose dependability is unknown cannot be regarded as dependable. In general, it will not be feasible to generate strong evidence for a system's dependability after it is built (but before deployment); the evidence will need to be produced as part of the development process. Beta-testing, controlled release, and other field-testing strategies may provide some evidence that software is acceptably dependable in applications that only require low dependability, but even in these less-critical applications, the evidence obtained through field-testing will rarely be sufficient to provide high confidence that the software has the required properties.

Goal-Based Versus Process-Based Assurance

To date, most approaches to developing dependable software (i.e., traditional approaches) have relied on fixed prescriptions, in which particular processes are applied and from which dependability is assumed to follow. The approach recommended in this report might be characterized in contrast as goal-based.

Even if a system has the same components and design as some other system, it is likely to be unique in its context of use and in the concerns of its stakeholders. For this reason, assurance for systems by reference to some fixed prescription is no longer advocated; instead, a goal-based approach is preferred. In a goal-based approach, the stakeholders first agree on the goals for which assurance is required (for example, "this device must not harm people"); then the developers produce specific claims (for example, "the radiation delivered by this device will never

---

[10]D.L. Parnas and J. Madey, 1995, "Functional documentation for computer systems," *Science of Computer Programming* 25(1):41-61.

[11]The view of requirements and specifications in this section is based on the work of Michael Jackson (2001, *Problem Frames: Analysing and Structuring Software Development Problems*, Addison-Wesley, Boston, Mass.; and 1996, *Software Requirements and Specifications*, Addison-Wesley and ACM Press, New York).

exceed so much intensity") and an argument to justify the claims based on verifiable evidence (for example, "there is a mechanical interlock on the beam intensity and here is evidence, derived from extensive testing, that it works"). The top levels of the argument will generally employ methods from systems thinking, such as hazard analysis, fault tree analysis, and failure modes and effects analysis, while lower levels will employ more specialized techniques appropriate to the system and technology concerned.

Process-based assurance will typically mandate (or strongly recommend) the processes that the developers must follow to support a claim for a particular level of dependability. For example, the avionics standard DO-178 mandates modified condition/decision coverage (MCDC) testing—described in Chapter 1—for the most critical software. This can lead to a culture where software producers follow the standard and then claim that their software has achieved the required dependability without providing any direct evidence that the resulting product actually has the required properties. In contrast, goal-based standards require the developers to state their dependability targets and to justify why these are adequate for the application, and then to choose development and assurance methods and to show how these methods provide sufficient evidence that the dependability targets have been achieved. Goal-based assurance will usually provide a far stronger dependability case than process-based assurance.

Another advantage of goal-based assurance cases over more prescriptive methods for assurance is that they allow expert developers to choose suitable solutions to novel design problems. In addition, goal-based assurance approaches are able to keep pace with technological change and with the attendant changes in system functions and hazards along with the goals of their stakeholders. As noted earlier, the increased flexibility demands expertise and judgment in discerning what technological and process approaches are best suited in a given circumstances to meet explicit requirements and develop the evidence needed for an ultimate dependability case.

In short, then, as explained above, the developers make explicit claims about the dependability properties of the delivered system. For these claims to be useful to the consumers of the system, the developers present, along with the claims, a dependability case arguing that the system has the claimed properties. Such an approach is only useful to the extent that the claims can be substantiated by the dependability case, and that the case is convincing. It therefore requires *transparency* so that the consumer (broadly construed) can assess the case's credibility and *accountability* to discourage misrepresentation.

The Dependability Case

Dependability requires justifiable confidence, which in turn requires that there be adequate evidence to support the claims of dependability, and that this evidence be available to those who have to assess the degree of confidence that the evidence supports. Claims for certifiably dependable software should therefore be not only explicit but also backed by sufficient evidence, and this evidence should be open to inspection and analysis by those assessing the dependability case.

What constitutes sufficient evidence for dependability depends on the nature of the claim and the degree of dependability that is required. In general, however, the evidence will constitute a dependability case that takes into account all components of the system as a whole: the software, physical devices with which it interacts, and assumptions about the domain in which it operates (which will usually include both assumptions about the physical environment and assumptions about the behavior of human operators).

Of course, the construction of those parts of the dependability case that go beyond the software may require skills and knowledge beyond those of the software engineer and may be relegated to domain experts. But it is vital that the software engineer still be responsible for ensuring not only that the part of the case involving software is sound, but also that it is used appropriately in the larger case.

The Role of Domain Assumptions

As explained in the preceding section, a dependability claim for a system should be made in terms of requirements that involve the phenomena of the environment; it is to affect these phenomena that the system is introduced in the first place. The software itself, on the other hand, is judged against a specification that involves only phenomena at the interface of the machine and the environment, which the software is capable of controlling directly.

Between the requirements and the specification lie domain assumptions. A dependability case will generally involve a statement of domain assumptions, along with their justifications, and an argument that the specification of the software and the domain assumptions together imply the requirements. Insisting on this tripartite division of responsibility—checking the software, checking the domain assumptions, and checking that they have the correct combined effect—is not a pedantry. As the Warsaw Airbus incident illustrates, the meeting point of these three components of the dependability case is often a system's Achilles' heel.

The Role of Architecture

The demand for evidence of dependability and the difficulty of producing such evidence for complex systems have a straightforward but profound implication. Any component for which compelling evidence of dependability has been constructed at reasonable cost will likely be small by the standards of most modern software systems. Every critical specification property, therefore, will have to be assured by one, or at most a few, small components. Sometimes it will not be possible to separate concerns so cleanly, and in that case, the dependability case will be less credible or more expensive to produce.

The case that the system satisfies a property has three parts:

• *An argument that the requirements properties will be satisfied by the specification of the system, in conjunction with the domain assumptions.* As explained above, this requires that the domain assumptions are made explicit and shown to be justified. For example, the specification of a controller that is used to maintain a safe level in a reservoir may depend on assumptions about signals from sensors, the behavior of valves, and the flow rate through outflow pipes under a range of operational conditions. These assumptions should be stated and reviewed by domain experts and may need to be tested under operational conditions to achieve the necessary confidence that they are correct.

• *An independence argument, based on architectural principles, that only certain components are relevant.* The independence argument will rely on properties of both the particular architecture and the language and implementation platform on which it stands. The easiest case will be where the components are physically separated, for example by running on separate processors with no shared memory. Where the components share memory, unless they use a safe, well-defined language and a robust, fully specified platform, such an argument will not be possible. For example, if the language allows arbitrary integers to be used as if they were pointers to variables (as in C), it will not be possible to argue that the regions of memory read and written by distinct modules are disjoint, so even modules implementing functionality unrelated to the property at issue would have to be treated as relevant. These shortcomings might be overcome, but only at considerable cost. For example, memory safety could be established by restricting the code to a subset that disallows certain constructs and then performing a review, preferably with the aid of automated tools, to ensure that the restriction has been obeyed.

• *A more detailed argument that the components behave appropriately.* This argument is likely to involve analysis of the specification for completeness and consistency, analysis of the design to show conformance with the specification, and analysis of the implemented software to show consistency with the design and the absence of unsafe properties (such as memory faults or the use of undefined values). The components, subsystems, and system will then usually be tested to provide some end-to-end assurance.

The degree of coupling between components, in the form of dependences that cause one component to rely on another, is likely to be a good indicator of the effort that will be required to construct a dependability argument. In general, the more dependences and the stronger the dependences, the more components will need to be considered and the more detailed their specifications will need to be, even to establish a limited property.

The Role of Testing

Testing is indispensable, and no software system can be regarded as dependable if it has not been extensively tested, even if its correctness has been proven mathematically. Testing can find flaws that elude analysis because it exercises the system in its entirety, where analysis must typically make assumptions about the execution platform that may turn out to be unwarranted. Human observation of an executing system, especially one that interacts heavily with a user, can also reveal serious flaws in the user interface, and even in the formulation of the dependability properties themselves.

Testing plays two distinct roles in software development. In the first role, testing is an integral component of the software development process. Automatic tests, run every time a change is made to the code, have proven to be extremely effective at catching faults unwittingly introduced during maintenance. If code is frequently refactored (that is, if code is modified to simplify its structure without changing its functionality) retesting is especially important. When a fault is found in the code, standard practice requires the construction of a regression test to ensure that the fault is not reintroduced later. Having programmers develop unit tests for their own modules encourages them to pay attention to specifications and can eliminate faults that would be more expensive to detect after integration. (There is some evidence, however, that unit tests are not particularly effective or necessary if code is developed from a formal specification and is subject to static analysis.[12])

Testing is often an inexpensive way to catch major flaws, especially in areas (such as user interfaces) where analysis is awkward. A skillfully

---

[12]S. King, J. Hammond, R. Chapman, and A. Pryor, eds. "Is proof more cost-effective than testing?" *IEEE Transactions on Software Engineering* 26(8):675-686.

constructed test suite can also find faults that would rarely fail in service but in ways difficult to diagnose; experienced programmers, for example, will insert diagnostics into concurrent code in patterns that are likely to expose data races and deadlocks. "Fuzz testing," in which a program is subjected to a huge suite of randomly generated test cases, often reveals faults that have escaped detection in other ways. The power of testing can be greatly amplified if formal models, even very partial ones, are available; tests can be generated automatically from state machine models using a technique known as "model-based testing" and from invariants or run-time assertions.

As Dijkstra observed, however, testing can reveal the presence of errors but not their absence.[13] The theoretical inadequacies of testing are well known. To test a program exhaustively would involve testing all possible inputs in all possible combinations and, if the program maintains any data from previous executions, all possible sequences of tests. This is clearly not feasible for most programs, and since software lacks the continuity of physical systems that allow inferences to be drawn from one sample execution about neighboring points, testing says little or nothing about the cases that were not exercised. Because state space[14] coverage is unattainable and hard even to measure, less ambitious forms of coverage have been invented, such as "all-statements" (in which every statement of the program must be executed at least once), "all-branches" (in which every branch in the control flow must be taken), and a variety of predicate coverage criteria (in which the aim is to achieve combinations of logical outcomes from the expressions that comprise the condition of each loop or if-statement). Testing researchers established early on that many of the intuitions that a tester might have that give confidence in the value of coverage are incorrect—for example, a coverage criterion that is stricter (in the sense that it rejects a larger set of test suites as inadequate) is not necessarily more effective at finding faults.[15] Moreover, a recent study showed that even the predicate coverage criterion known as MCDC (used

---

[13]O. Dahl, E.W. Dijkstra, and C.A. Hoare, 1972, *Structured Programming*, Academic Press, New York.

[14]The "state space" of a system is the set of states—internal configurations or conditions— that the system can potentially occupy. If a test suite covers the entire state space, then every possible configuration has been tested, and the test is complete. In practice, however, the state space is usually so large that only a small proportion is exercised by a test suite. Model-based testing is an approach that seeks to appropriately abstract and consolidate states in meaningful ways so that more of the state space can be covered. Demonstrating the appropriateness of the abstraction and consolidation then becomes another element of the construction of the dependability case.

[15]Phyllis G. Frankl and Elaine J. Weyuker, 1993, "A formal analysis of the fault-detecting ability of testing methods," *IEEE Transactions in Software Engineering* 19(3):202-213.

widely in avionics and regarded as extremely burdensome) does not ensure the detection of a class of bugs found easily by static analysis.[16]

As Hoare has noted,[17] testing is, in practice, "more effective than it has any right to be" in improving the quality and dependability of software. Hoare's explanation is that while the contribution of testing to exposing bugs might only account for low levels of dependability, its contribution to providing feedback on the development process might account for much higher levels. In Hoare's words: "The real value of tests is not that they detect bugs in the code but that they detect inadequacies in the methods, concentration, and skills of those who design and produce the code." The most conscientious development teams indeed use testing in this manner. When a module or subsystem fails too many tests, the developers do not simply attempt to patch the code. Instead, they look to the development process to determine where the error was introduced that eventually resulted in the failure, and they make the correction there. This might involve clarifying requirements or specifications, reworking a design, recoding one or more modules from scratch, and, in extreme cases, abandoning the entire development and starting afresh.

In short, testing is a powerful and indispensable tool, and a development that lacks systematic testing should not be regarded as acceptable in any professional setting, let alone for critical systems. How a software supplier uses testing is important information in assessing the credibility of its dependability claims (see the discussion of transparency in Chapter 3).

The second role of testing is in providing concrete evidence that can be used in a dependability case. Testing is an essential complement to analysis. Because the activities of testing differ so markedly from those involved in analysis, testing provides important redundancy and can catch mistakes made during the analysis process, whether by humans or tools. The dependability case for an extrinsic property will often rely on assumptions about a physical device, which will be represented as a formal model for the purpose of analysis. Such formal models should obviously be tested—ideally before they are used as the basis for development. A patient monitoring system, for example, might assume certain properties of accuracy and responsiveness for the monitoring devices; the case for the system as a whole will require these to be substantiated by extensive and rigorous testing, ideally not only by the suppliers of the

---

[16]Andy German and Gavin Mooney, 2001, "Air vehicle software static code analysis—Lessons learnt," *Proceedings of the Ninth Safety-Critical Systems Symposium*, Felix Redmill and Tom Anderson, eds., Springer-Verlag, Bristol, United Kingdom.

[17]C.A.R. Hoare, 1996, "How did software get so reliable without proof?" *Lecture Notes in Computer Science* 1051:1-17.

devices but also by the developers of the system that uses them. End-to-end tests are especially important to catch interactions and couplings that may not have been predicted. In a radiotherapy system, for example, the beam would be examined with a dosimeter to ensure that the physical dose delivered at the nozzle matches the prescribed dose entered earlier at the therapist's workstation.

At the same time, it is important to realize that testing alone is very rarely sufficient to establish high levels of dependability. Testing will be an essential component of a dependability case but will not in general suffice, because even the largest test suites typically used will not exercise enough paths to provide evidence that the software is correct and have little statistical significance for the levels of confidence usually desired. It is erroneous to believe that a rigorous development process in which testing and code review are the only verification techniques would justify claims of extraordinarily high levels of dependability. Some certification schemes, for example, associate higher "safety integrity levels" with more burdensome process prescriptions and imply that following the processes recommended for the highest integrity levels gives confidence that the failure rate will be less than 1 failure per 1 billion hours. Such claims have no scientific basis.

Furthermore, unless a system is very small or has been meticulously developed bearing in mind the construction of a dependability case, credible claims of dependability are usually impossible or impractically expensive to demonstrate after design and development of the system have been completed.[18]

Another form of evidence that is widely used in dependability claims for a component or system to be used in a critical setting is its prior extensive use. In fact, the internal state space of a complex software system may be so large that even several years' worth of execution by millions of users cannot be assumed to achieve complete coverage. A new environment might expose unknown vulnerabilities in a component. Components designed for use in commercial, low-criticality contexts are not suitable for critical settings unless justified by an explicit dependability case that places only appropriate weight on previous successful uses.

Testing offered as part of a dependability case, like all other components of the dependability case, should be carefully justified. Since the purpose of the dependability case is to establish the critical properties of the system, the degree of confidence warranted by the testing will vary

---

[18]B. Littlewood and L. Strigini, 1993, "Validation of ultra-high dependability for software-based systems," *Communications of the ACM* 36(11):69-80. Also see R. Butler and G. Finelli, 1993, "The infeasibility of quantifying the reliability of life-critical real-time software," *IEEE Transactions on Software Engineering* 19(1):3-12.

according to the strength of the connection between the tests and the properties claimed. At one extreme, if a component can be tested exhaustively for all possible inputs, testing becomes tantamount to proof, giving very high confidence. At the other extreme, execution of even a large set of end-to-end tests, even if it achieves high levels of code coverage, in itself says little about the dependability of the system as a whole.

It cannot be stressed too much that for testing to be a credible component of a dependability case, the relationship between testing and the properties claimed will need to be explicitly justified. The tester may appeal to known properties of the internals of the system or to a statistical analysis involving the system's operational profile. In many cases, the justification will necessarily involve an argument based on experience—for example, that attaining a certain coverage level has in the past led to certain measured failure rates. That experience should be carefully evaluated. Sometimes, the test suite itself may be treated as direct evidence for dependability. For a standard test suite (such as the Java Compatibility Kit used for testing implementations of the Java platform[19]), it will be possible to base the degree of confidence on the opinions of experts familiar with the suite. But a custom test suite, however credible, may place an unreasonable burden on those assessing the dependability case.

Until major advances are made, therefore, testing should be regarded in general as only a limited means of finding flaws, and the evidence of a clean testing run should carry weight in a dependability argument only to the extent that its implications for critical properties can be explicitly justified.

The Role of Analysis

Because testing alone is insufficient, for the foreseeable future the dependability claim will also require evidence produced by analysis. Moreover, because analysis links the software artifacts directly to the claimed properties, for the highest levels of dependability, the analysis component of the dependability case will usually contribute confidence at lower cost.

Analysis may involve well-reasoned informal argument, formal proofs of code correctness, and mechanical inference (as performed, for example, by "type checkers" that confirm that every use of each variable in a program is consistent with the properties that the variables were defined to have). Indeed, the dependability case for even a relatively simple system will usually require all of these kinds of analysis, and they will need to be fitted together into a coherent whole.

---

[19]For more information on the Java Compatibility Kit, see <https://jck.dev.java.net/>.

Type checking, for example, may be used to establish the independence of modules; known properties of the operating system may be used to justify the assumption that address space separation is sound; modular correctness proofs used to establish that, under these assumptions, the software satisfies its intrinsic specifications; and informal argument, perhaps augmented with some formal reasoning, to make the link to the crucial extrinsic properties.

An argument taking the form of a chain of reasoning cannot be stronger than its weakest link. (Recent research[20] on combining diverse arguments opens the possibility that independent, weak arguments for the dependability of a system could some day be combined to provide a quantifiably stronger argument.) It will therefore be necessary to ensure that the tools and notations used to construct and check the argument are robust. If they are not, extraordinary efforts will be required to overcome their limitations. For example, if a language is used that does not require that the allowable properties of every program object are tightly defined and enforced (i.e., a "type-unsafe" or "weakly typed" language), a separate, explicit argument will need to be constructed to ensure that there are no violations of memory discipline that would compromise modular reasoning. If the programming language has constructs that are not precisely defined, or that result in compiler-dependent behavior, it will be necessary to restrict programmers to a suitable subset that is immune to the known problems.

As noted in Chapter 1, there are difficulties and limits to contemporary software analysis methods, owing in part to the need for a highly trained and competent software development staff. Indeed, the quality of the staff is at least as important as the development methods and tools that are used, and so these factors should also be included in the evidence.

Rigorous Process: Preserving the Chain of Evidence

Although it might be possible to construct a dependability case after the fact, in practice it will probably only be achievable if the software is built with the dependability case in mind. Each step in developing the software needs to preserve the chain of evidence on which will be based the argument that the resulting system is dependable.

At the start, the domain assumptions and the required properties of the system should be made explicit; they should be expressed unambigu-

---

[20]For example, Robin Bloomfield and Bev Littlewood, 2006, "On the use of diverse arguments to increase confidence in dependability claims," in *Structure for Dependability*, D. Besnard, C. Gacek, and C.B. Jones, eds., Springer-Verlag, New York, pp. 254-268.

ously and in a form that permits systematic analysis to ensure that there are no unresolvable conflicts between the required properties. Because each subsequent stage of development should preserve the evidence chain that these properties have been carried forward without being corrupted, each form in which the design or implementation requirements are expressed should support sufficient checking that the required properties have been preserved.

What is sufficient will vary with the required dependability, but preserving the evidence chain necessitates that the checks are carried out in a disciplined way, following a documented procedure and leaving auditable records—in other words, a rigorous process. For example, if the dependability argument relies, in part, on reasoning from the properties of components, then the system build process should leave evidence that the system has been built out of the specific versions of each component for which there is evidence that the component has the necessary properties. This can be thought of as "rigorous configuration management."

Components and Reuse

Complex components are seldom furnished with the information needed to support dependability arguments for the systems that use them. For use within a larger argument, the details of the dependability case of a component need not be known (and might involve proprietary details of the component's design). But the claims made for a component should be known and clearly understood, and it should be possible to assess their credibility by, for example, the reputation of a third-party reviewer (in much the same way as the FAA credibly assures the airworthiness of aircraft) or the nature of the evidence.

Not all systems and not all properties are equally critical, and not all the components in a system need assurance to the same level: for example, we may demand that one component can fail to satisfy some property no more than one time in a billion, while for another property we might tolerate one failure in a thousand. Until recently, there has been little demand for components to be delivered with the claims, argument, and evidence needed to support the dependability case for a system that uses the component. At lower levels of criticality, and in accidental systems, explicit dependability cases have seldom been constructed, so there has been no perceived need for component-level cases. At the other extreme, systems with highly critical assurance goals (such as airplanes) have driven their dependability cases down into the details of their components and have lacked regulatory mechanisms to support use of prequalified critical components, which would allow the case for the larger system to use the case for its components without inquiring into all the details of the components themselves.

With greater reuse of components, and a concomitant awareness of the risks involved (especially of using commodity operating systems in critical settings), component-level assurance will become an essential activity throughout the industry. In the case of critical systems such as airplanes, it used to be the case that their software was built on highly idiosyncratic platforms that were seldom reused from one airplane to the next, and the same was true of the architectural frameworks that tie multiple computer systems and buses together to support fault-tolerant functions such as autopilot, autoland, flight management, and so on. Nowadays, however, the software is generally built on real-time operating systems such as LynxOS-178 that are highly specialized but nonetheless standardized components, and standardized architectural frameworks such as Primus Epic and the Time-Triggered Architecture (TTA) have emerged to support Integrated Modular Avionics (IMA).

To support these developments, the FAA developed an advisory circular on reusable software components,[21] and guidelines for IMA have been developed by the appropriate technical bodies (SC200 of RTCA and WG60 of EUROCAE) and are currently being voted on. Both of these developments are rather limited, however, in that they allow only for a software component that has been used in the traditional assurance case for a certified airplane to take the assurance data developed in that certification into the assurance case for additional airplanes; they fall short of allowing the assurance case for a system to build on the assurance cases for its components.

In the case of less-critical systems, much attention has been focused recently on the use of commercial off-the-shelf (COTS) subsystems and software of uncertain pedigree/unknown provenance (SOUP). While the attention has focused mostly on the use of architectural mechanisms (for example, wrappers) to mitigate the unknown (un)reliability of these components, it has also highlighted the lack of assurance data for these components: It matters less that they are unreliable than that it is unknown how unreliable they are, and in what ways their unreliability is manifested.

Accidental systems often use COTS and SOUP and do so in contexts that promote criticality creep (see previous discussion). If these cases were recognized appropriately as systems and subjected to an appropriate dependability regime, the cost of providing adequate dependability

---

[21]Federal Aviation Administration (FAA), 2004, "Reusable software components," AC 20-148, FAA, Washington, D.C. Available online at <http://www.airweb.faa.gov/Regulatory_and_Guidance_Library/rgAdvisoryCircular.nsf/0/EBFCCB29C0E78FFF86256F6300617BDD?OpenDocument>.

evidence for the COTS/SOUP component might exceed the cost of developing a new component when high dependability is required.

It is apparent that at all levels of criticality it is currently impossible to develop dependability cases for systems based solely on those cases for their components. In the case of critical systems such as airplanes this is mostly because the regulatory framework does not allow it, in part because the science base does not yet provide the ability to reason about system-level properties such as safety or security based solely on the properties of the system's components. In the case of less critical and accidental systems, it is often because such systems rely on COTS and SOUP, for which no suitable assurance data are available.

EXPERTISE

Building software is hard; building dependable software is harder. Although the approach advocated in this report is designed to be as free as possible from the fetters of particular technologies, it also assumes that developers are using the very best techniques and tools available. A development team that is unfamiliar and inexperienced with best practices is very unlikely to succeed.

This section therefore contains an outline of some of today's best practices. It might be used in many ways: for educational planning, for assessing development organizations, for evaluating potential recruits, and even as the basis for licensing. However, the committee offers the outline only as guidance and would not want it to be seen as binding in all circumstances. Few best practices have universal application, and most need to be adjusted to the context of a particular problem.

Different problems and different development contexts call for different practices. Moreover, what is considered to be best practice changes over time, as new languages and tools appear and ideas about how to develop software continue to mature. The committee therefore felt it would be unwise to tie its recommendations to particular practices. In addition, merely applying a set of best practices absent a carefully constructed dependability case does not warrant confidence in the system's dependability.

At the same time, in order to make concrete the importance of best practices, the committee decided to offer a list of practices that it regards as representative of a broad consensus at the time of writing. It also seemed desirable to provide some guidance regarding today's best practices, especially since developers in smaller organizations are often unaware of simple practices that can dramatically improve software quality.

This section begins with a discussion of simplicity, because a commitment to simplicity is key to achieving justifiable confidence and depend-

able software. A commitment to simplicity is often the mark of true expertise. The list of particular best practices that follows this discussion is
by no means exhaustive. It represents the consensus of the committee
on a core set of practices that can be widely applied and that can bring
dramatic benefit at relatively low cost. For the most part, these practices
represent minimal standards of software engineering. In some cases, for
development of a noncritical system in which high dependablity is not
required, less stringent practices may make sense, as noted in the list.

Simplicity

> The price of reliability is the pursuit of the utmost simplicity. It is a price
> which the very rich find most hard to pay.[22]

In practice, the key to achieving dependability at reasonable cost is
a serious and sustained commitment to simplicity. An awareness of the
need for simplicity usually comes only with bitter experience and the
humility gained from years of practice. Moreover, the ability to achieve
simplicity likewise comes from experience. As Alan Perlis said, "Simplicity does not precede complexity, but follows it."[23]

The most important form of simplicity is that produced by independence, in which particular system-level properties are guaranteed
by individual components, much smaller than the system as a whole,
whose preservation of these properties is immune to failures in the rest
of the system. Independence can be established in the overall design of
the system with the support of architectural mechanisms. Its effect is to
dramatically reduce the cost of constructing a dependability case for a
property, since only a relatively small part of the system needs to be considered. Where independence is not possible, well-formed dependence is
critical. Independence allows the isolation of safe critical functions to a
small number of components. Well-formed dependence (wherein a less-
critical service may depend on a critical service but not vice versa) allows
critical services to be safely used by the rest of the system. Independence
and well-formed dependence are important design principles of overall
system architecture. Simplicity has wider applications, however, which
the rest of this section discusses.

A major attraction of software as an implementation medium is its
capacity for complexity. Functions that are hard, expensive, or impossible

---

[22]C.A.R. Hoare, 1981, "The emperor's old clothes" (Turing Award Lecture), *Communications of the ACM* 24(2):75-83. Available online at <http://portal.acm.org/citation.
cfm?id=358561>.

[23]Alan J. Perlis, 1982, "Epigrams on programming," *SIGPLAN Notices* 17(9):7-13.

to implement by other means (whether automatically in physical devices or manually in human organizations) can often be realized at low cost in software. Indeed, the marginal cost of complexity in software can seem negligible, as the cost of computational resources drops. In fact, however, complexity can inflict large costs. When a software system grows as new and more complex functions are added, its structure tends to deteriorate, and each new modification becomes harder to perform, requiring more parts of the code to be changed. It is not uncommon for a system to collapse under the weight of its own complexity.[24]

Developers usually cannot shield the user from the complexity of software. As the specification becomes more complex, it typically loses any coherence it once possessed. The user has no intelligible conceptual model of the system's behavior and can obtain predictable results only by sticking to well-tried scenarios.

Complexity has, of course, a legitimate role. After all, software is often used precisely to satisfy the need for complex functions that are more cheaply and reliably implemented by software than by other means, mechanical or human. But complexity exacts a heavy price. The more complex a system is, the less well it is understood by its developers and the harder it is to test, review, and analyze. Moreover, complex systems are likely to consist of complex individual components. Complex individual components are more likely to fail individually than simpler components and more likely to suffer from unanticipated interactions. These interactions are most serious amongst systems and between systems and their human users; in many accidents (for example, at Three Mile Island[25]), users unwittingly took a system toward catastrophe because they were unable to understand what the system was doing.

Whether a system's complexity is warranted is, of course, a difficult judgment, and systems serving more users and offering more powerful functionality will generally be more complex. Moreover, the demand for dependability itself tends to increase complexity in some areas. For example, a system may require a very robust storage facility for its data. This will inevitably make the system more complex than one in which data loss can be tolerated. But the lesson of simplicity still applies, and a designer committed to simplicity would choose, for example, a standard replication scheme over a more complicated and ad hoc design that attempts to exploit the particular properties of the data.

---

[24]The failure of Netscape, for example, has been attributed in part to the company's inability to extricate itself from the complexity of its Navigator browser. See Michael A. Cusumano and David B. Yoffie, 1998, *Competing on Internet Time: Lessons from Netscape and Its Battle with Microsoft*, Free Press, New York.

[25]See Charles Perrow, 1999, *Normal Accidents*, Princeton University Press, Princeton, N.J.

The overriding importance of simplicity in software development has been championed for decades. Formal methods researchers, such as Hoare (quoted above), were among the first to stress its value because they discovered early that extra complexity rapidly destroys the ability to generate evidence for dependability. Many practitioners have argued that the complexity of software is inherent to the task at hand, but this position has eroded, and views such as those reflected in the dicta of agile methodologies—"you aren't gonna need it" and "the simplest thing that works"—are gaining ground.

There is no alternative to simplicity. Advances in technology or development methods will not make simplicity redundant; on the contrary, they will give it greater leverage. To achieve high levels of dependability in the foreseeable future, striving for simplicity is likely to be by far the most cost-effective of all interventions. Simplicity is not easy or cheap, but its rewards far outweigh its costs.

Here are some examples of how a commitment to simplicity can be demonstrated throughout the stages of a development:

• *Requirements.* A development should start with a carefully chosen, minimal set of requirements. Complex features often exact a cost that greatly exceeds the benefit they bring to users. The key to simplicity in requirements is the construction of abstractions and generalizations that allow simple, uniform functions to be used for multiple purposes. Over-generalization, of course, can itself be a source of gratuitous complexity but can usually be recognized because it makes the requirements more, not less, complicated.

• *Architecture.* Small and simple components are easier to reason about and less likely to harbor subtle bugs. Simple and clean interfaces reduce the risk of misunderstandings between members of the development team and reduce the incidence of complex interactions, which are the most common cause of bugs in large systems. It is a mistake to believe that richer interfaces with a larger array of more elaborate functions benefit the users of the interface; on the contrary, they tend to be less useful and perform more poorly.[26] A dependence graph of the code showing which other modules each module depends on can reveal sources of architectural complexity, indicating where layering is violated, where low-level modules depend on high-level ones, where cycles prevent modular reasoning, or where simply a proliferation of dependences suggests a breakdown of the original design.

---

[26]Butler Lampson, 1983, "Hints for computer system design," *ACM Operating Systems Review* 17(5):33-48. (Reprinted in *IEEE Software* 1(1):11-28. Available online at <http://research.microsoft.com/lampson/33-Hints/WebPage.html>.)

• *Trusted base.* If the dependability properties of a system can be confined to a small trusted base consisting of only a few components so that the properties can be guaranteed without analyzing the rest of the system (except perhaps to establish certain noninterference properties), powerful techniques such as program verification, which would not be feasible for the system as a whole, can be applied locally to provide a level of confidence not attainable by any other means.

• *Languages.* Complex development languages can undermine a development by making even a simple design appear complex and by introducing new opportunities for error. Developers should be wary of complex and poorly defined modeling languages[27] and of programming languages with imprecise semantics, or semantics that are platform- or compiler-dependent. When other factors dictate the use of an overly complex language, simplicity can often be regained by restricting usage to a well-defined and robust subset (such as the SPARK subset of Ada).[28]

• *Tools.* Developers should favor simple tools and should be especially wary of code generation tools whose behavior is poorly understood. Tools that perform elaborate functions may need to be complex, but understanding how to use them and assessing their output should not be complex. A code verification tool, for example, might have complex analysis functions, but it should report its results in an intelligible fashion and, ideally, produce a proof that can be independently checked by a simpler tool.

• *Process.* A rigorous process is essential to constructing a dependability case, but an elaborate and complex process that places a heavy burden on developers can be worse than no process at all. Excessive documentation is particularly problematic; it diverts attention from more important matters and is usually write-only. A common tendency is to set elaborate standards in trivial areas: Some organizations, for example, have coding standards that specify meticulously how various constructs should be formatted (a task that should be carried out by an editing tool) but fail to address the major weaknesses of the programming language.

---

[27]In computer science and allied fields of information management and business process modeling, modeling languages enable software architects, business analysts, and others to specify the requirements of an organizational or software system on a "top" or architectural level. These languages seek to diagrammatically render system requirements in a manner that management, user groups, and other stakeholders can understand, with the goal of eliciting feedback from these groups.

[28]John Barnes, 2003, *High Integrity Software: The SPARK Approach to Safety and Security,* Addison-Wesley, Boston, Mass.

Best Practices

The following subsections describe some of today's specific system-level, code- and module-level, and process-level best practices.

System-Level Practices

The committee offers a set of system-level best practices below.

- *Prioritization of requirements.* Prioritize requirements and articulate them simply and directly in terms of key properties rather than as a long list of functions, features, or scenarios.
- *Requirements vs. specifications.* The requirements of a software system should describe the intended effect of the system on its environment and not, more narrowly, the behavior of the system at its interface with the environment, which is the subject of the specification.
- *Realistic demands.* Do not include requirements that are unrealistic or that cannot be realistically assessed. In particular, vague numerical measures are not a substitute for precise requirements: The requirement of "six 9s availability," for example, makes little sense without a clear articulation of which service is being provided and what constitutes availability or lack thereof.
- *Environmental assumptions.* In the requirements document, clearly separate the demands on the software system being constructed from the demands on the environment or its operators. Include an explicit description of the environment, with a glossary that covers the domain-specific terms used throughout the document. Articulate precisely and fully any environmental assumptions and have them reviewed by domain experts.
- *Hazard analysis.* For a critical application, perform a hazard analysis that identifies the most likely hazards and checks that they have been mitigated appropriately. Address security risks by building and evaluating explicit threat models.
- *Dependability case.* For a critical application, construct a dependability case that explains why the system executing in context is likely to satisfy the prioritized requirements.
- *Usability testing.* Apply usability testing to user interfaces in the early phases of development and periodically from then on.
- *Formal modeling and analysis.* Express requirements and specifications precisely and unambiguously. An effective way to do this is to use a formal notation. For a noncritical system, a complete formal model will not generally be cost-effective, but it will usually be feasible and desirable to express at least the most important elements formally.
- *Analysis tools.* Exploit automatic analysis tools to find defects in requirements and specifications documents and to increase confidence in

their correctness. In noncritical developments this may involve little more than using tools that check for consistent use of names. In critical developments, use tools that offer deeper analysis, such as model checkers and simulators.

• *Standard solutions.* Adopt standard solutions for algorithms and protocols unless a strong case has been made for deviating from standard practice. Avoid inventing algorithms in areas that are known to be extremely hard to design correctly (for example, distributed consensus, authentication, fault tolerance). If the standard solution seems not to apply, consult an expert.

Code- and Module-Level Practices

Other best practices would apply at the code and module levels:

• *Interfaces.* Design interfaces between modules that are small and well-defined. Exploit programming language mechanisms to express the module structure and check it at compile time. Specify all public interfaces fully and integrate the specifications with the code, using, for example, a tool such as Javadoc.[29]

• *Data abstraction.* Minimize the scope and accessibility of all program components. Hide the representation of data using data abstraction, and use programming language mechanisms to enforce it. Make data types immutable whenever possible.

• *Inheritance.* Inheritance is a powerful but dangerous programming feature. Use it sparingly, and whenever possible favor composition (adding functionality by embedding one object explicitly in another) over inheritance. Design for inheritance or prohibit it, and do not extend classes that were not designed with extension in mind. In critical applications, avoid inheritance or ensure that adequate time has been allowed for the extensive additional verification activity that will be required.

• *Module dependences.* Evaluate the code structure by constructing a module dependence diagram (preferably with an automated tool), and modify the code to eliminate complex or troublesome dependences (especially those violating layering, and those forming cycles).

• *Standard libraries.* Use standard libraries unless (1) sufficiently robust libraries are not available for the functionality desired or (2) a much smaller and simpler library can be constructed for the problem at hand using published and peer-reviewed algorithms.

---

[29]For more information about the Javadoc tool, see <http://java.sun.com/j2se/javadoc/>.

- *Safe language.* Use a safe programming language where feasible and exploit the features that amplify static type checking (such as generics). Avoid extralinguistic or borderline features (such as native methods, reflection, and serialization). Know and avoid the traps and pitfalls of the platform. For a critical application, consider using a robust subset of the language (e.g., MISRA-C and SPARK); using an unsafe language (such as C) is unacceptable unless extraordinary measures (such as proof of type correctness) have been taken to mitigate the risks.[30]
- *Coding standards.* Establish clear and simple coding standards to enforce good practices in the use of programming language features.[31] Conventions for naming and layout are useful, especially because they amplify the power of simple lexical tools, but they are secondary to standards that have a direct impact on dependability. Appropriate coding standards are especially effective at eliminating security vulnerabilities.
- *Defensive programming.* Make liberal use of runtime assertions to detect flaws in the code and incorrect environmental assumptions, and disable them in the deployed code only after careful consideration. Assertions that embody preconditions, postconditions, and representation invariants are especially effective.
- *Logging failures.* Generate a log of messages that record in detail the circumstances of any detected failure that occurs at runtime. The message log should be examined frequently even if there are no serious failures and should be archived for later analysis.
- *Testing.* Automate testing, especially for regressions. Use tools to measure test coverage and aim to achieve full coverage of all statements.

---

[30]Almost all programming languages that are currently used in industry permit the programmer to write syntactically correct programs whose meaning is uncertain. In C, for example, the language standard allows the order in which the compiled code evaluates the individual elements of an expression to change each time the program is compiled. If an expression contains a function call, and the function changes the value of a variable that is also used in the expression, the value of the expression will depend on the order of evaluation, and the meaning of the program is undefined and may change following a recompilation. Some language standards attempt to resolve the problem of undefined programs by declaring them illegal but leave the compiler writer helpless to tell the programmer that their program is illegal before it is executed. For example, if an attempt is made to store a value in the 11th cell of an array defined in the C language to have 10 elements, the program is illegal and its behavior is undefined, but this will not be detected before the program is executed. This weakness in C is at the heart of the notorious "buffer overflows" that create the security vulnerabilities that have been exploited by many viruses and worms. When a programming language standard allows legal programs to have an undefined meaning, or where it declares certain programs to be illegal but the illegality cannot practically be determined before the program is executed, the programming language is said to be "unsafe."

[31]For a good example of a small collection of well-justified and easy-to-apply rules, see G.J. Holzmann, 2006, "The power of ten: Rules for developing safety critical code," *IEEE Computer* 39(6):95-97.

Every method of an exported application programming interface (API) should be tested. Do not regard testing as a tool to eliminate errors; instead, regard it as a quality control tool, and discard software that contains significant numbers of errors. Change the design if necessary to make thorough testing feasible.

• *Static analysis.* The compiler should be used in its strictest mode, and all code should pass without warnings. Use a static analysis tool to detect anomalies in the code; several such tools are now readily available. Specialized static analyses can establish the absence of certain kinds of security vulnerabilities.

• *Code review.* Conduct systematic reviews of all code as early as possible, before the code is placed in the project repository.

• *Incremental build.* Integrate the code of a system early and often. Include all checking tools in the automatic build process, including static analyses, unit and regression tests, and dependency analyses.

Process-Level Practices

Best practices at the process level include the following:

• *Process.* A robust and clear quality management system that is appropriate to the development organization and the character of the software being developed should be chosen, documented, and adhered to. Individuals should be trained in the aspects of the system that are relevant to their roles, and the process should encompass verification that its requirements are being adhered to and a systematic effort to review the costs and benefits of the process and improve it as appropriate.[32]

• *Risk management.* Identify key risks (of failure in development or failures of the product), record them in a risk register (essentially a table of all known risks), and articulate a plan to mitigate them. An incremental approach is most likely to succeed, focusing on major risks early on, developing core features first (including those that will have a significant impact on product architecture), and minimizing complexity.

• *Project planning.* The project should have an explicit plan with milestones against which progress is systematically evaluated. The plan should explicitly address the risks identified in the risk register.

• *Quality planning.* The project should have an explicit quality plan that articulates the quality criteria and describes how the quality criteria will be achieved and how the product will be assessed against them.

---

[32]Key processes that should be defined include specification, design, programming, version control, risk management, reviewing, testing, management of subcontractors, contract reviews, and documentation. ISO standard 9000-3 provides an example of this sort of process definition and management.

• *Version control.* All of the significant project documents (requirements, designs, code, plans, reports, and so on) should contain a date, version number, and change history and be kept under strict version control. In particular, a standard source code control system should be used that provides versioning, backup, and conflict detection.

• *Bug tracking.* All reported bugs should be documented in a database and indexed against the location where they were discovered in the code, design, or other documentation. All bug fixes should be fully documented and indexed against the appropriate bug report, and should result in reverification, including reexecution of regression test suites and the creation of new regression test cases. In any important application, each bug should be traced to its origin in the development, and a review should ensue to determine whether there are other similar bugs and what modifications to the development process could reduce the likelihood of such bugs occurring in the future.

• *Phased delivery.* Deliver a system in phases, with the most basic and important functions delivered in the first phase and additional functions delivered in later phases, in order to exploit feedback from users and reduce risk.

• *Independent review.* In a critical application, reviews by the development team should be augmented by reviews by an independent party.

FEASIBILITY OF THE OVERALL APPROACH

The approach to justifiable confidence and dependable software proposed in this chapter and the technical practices it involves should be adoptable without significant risk, because the practices have already been successfully applied by a few companies, as illustrated by the four papers cited in the next three paragraphs.

The importance of taking a systems perspective and regarding the direct human users of the computer interface as part of the overall system is widely recognized—in the aviation industry, for example, the aircraft is seen as a single system and the likelihood of error by the pilot is a factor treated explicitly in the system design and in safety analysis and certification. The importance of simplicity, even in complex applications, has long been understood in high-security systems, where the software that protects data integrity and confidentiality is kept as simple as possible and often implemented as a "security kernel." An example is described in a paper in *IEEE Software.*[33]

The benefits of exploiting analysis in addition to testing have been demonstrated on several projects reported in the literature. A good analy-

---

[33]R. Chapman and A. Hall, 2002, "Correctness by construction: Developing a commercially secure system," *IEEE Software* (January/February):18-25.

sis of a number of commercial projects is contained in a paper in *IEEE Transactions on Software Engineering.*[34] The importance and effectiveness of capturing environmental assumptions is explained with reference to an e-commerce system, a safety protection system, and a railway signaling system in a 2001 conference report.[35]

Evidence-based dependability cases and explicit claims are widely used in safety-critical software development but have also been shown to be cost-effective when building commercial applications.[36] The common experience, from these reports and others, is that these technical recommendations are practical to adopt and effective in use by experts. As with all engineering, cost-effectiveness is a primary objective; making dependability claims explicit allows developers to ensure that they achieve the necessary dependability without overengineering.

---

[34]S. King, J. Hammond, R. Chapman, and A. Pryor, 2000, "Is proof more cost-effective than testing?" *IEEE Transactions on Software Engineering* 26(8):675-686.

[35]J. Hammond, R. Rawlings, and A. Hall, 2001, "Will it work?" *Proceedings of the 5th IEEE International Symposium on Requirements Engineering*, August.

[36]Adrian Hilton, 2003, "Engineering Software Systems for Customer Acceptance." Available online at <http://www.praxis-his.co.uk/pdfs/customer_acceptance.pdf>.

3

Broader Issues

The preceding chapter outlined a comprehensive approach to the development of certifiably dependable software. The proposed approach has implications not only for how software is produced and evaluated but also for government policy, legislation, and regulation; education; and research. Each of these areas warrants in-depth studies of its own, and the committee recognizes that policy prescriptions in particular—especially in light of the limited data and evidence available in the arena of certifiably dependable software—can have complex and unpredictable ramifications. The committee has therefore chosen to refrain from making concrete and prescriptive recommendations aimed at particular agencies or specific domains. Nevertheless, it seemed useful to outline some of the relevant issues and note areas for further investigation and consideration.

TRANSPARENCY

Dependable systems need dependable components, tools, and software companies, so it is important that customers and users be able to make an informed judgment when choosing suppliers and products. This only becomes possible when the criteria and evidence underlying claims of dependability are transparent.

Economists have established that if consumers cannot reliably observe quality before they buy, then sellers may get little economic benefit from providing higher quality than their competitors, and overall quality can decline.[1] Because their reputation will affect future sales, sellers strive to maintain some minimum level of quality. If consumers rely heavily on such branding, though, it becomes more difficult for new firms to enter the market. In this case, the software industry could lose out on quality or other improvements because new and innovative firms had limited means of proving their quality. Information asymmetries of this type can be mitigated if dependability claims are explicit and backed by evidence, as long as the evidence is available for inspection by potential buyers.

Such transparency, in which those claiming dependability for their software make available the details of their claims, criteria, and evidence, is thus essential for providing the correct market conditions under which informed choices can be made and the more dependable suppliers can prosper.

To assess the credibility of such details effectively, an evaluator should be able to calibrate not only the technical claims and evidence but also the organization that produced them, because the integrity of the evidence chain is vital and cannot easily be assessed without supporting data. This suggests that data of a more general nature should be made available, including the qualifications of the personnel involved in the development; the track record of the organization in providing dependable software, which might include, for example, defect rates on previous projects; and the process by which the software was developed and the dependability argument constructed, which might include process manuals and metrics, internal standards documents, applicable test suites and results, and tools used.

A company is likely to be reluctant to reveal data that might be of benefit to a competitor or that might tarnish the company's reputation. It is also likely that demands to publish defect rates would result in careful redefinitions of what constitutes a defect. These concerns, however, should not deter users from demanding such information, but the demands should be reasonable, well-defined, and commensurate with the dependability claimed and the consequences of failure. The willingness of a supplier to provide such data, and the clarity and integrity of the data that it provides, will be a strong indication of its attitude toward dependability, since a supplier who truly understands the role of evidence in establishing dependability will be eager to provide such evidence, and a supplier who does not understand the need for evidence is unlikely to understand all the other attributes of dependability.

One would not expect the users of a commodity operating system for standard office purposes to press for such information, although it would

---

[1]See, for example, George A. Akerlof, 1970, "The market for 'lemons': Quality uncertainty and the market mechanism," *Quarterly Journal of Economics* 84:488-500.

be reasonable to expect lists of all known defects, details of the rate at which new defects were reported, and the rate of repair. In contrast, however, the public might reasonably demand that very detailed information about the construction and validation of an electronic voting system be made publicly available. Similarly, patients who receive treatment from a potentially lethal medical device should have access to information about its evaluation just as they have access to information about the side effects and risks of medications.

It should be noted that providing direct access to evidence is not the only way that a supplier can signal quality. More widespread use of warranties, for example, would help consumers select the more dependable products and suppliers, so long as the warranties are based on explicit claims about the properties of the software and are not simply a marketing gimmick. Industry practice with regard to warranties on commercial software varies widely, with some software developers continuing to disclaim all responsibility for the quality of their products and some routinely warranting turnkey systems against all defects.

At the same time, consumer confidence is not necessarily a good measure of quality. Research into the effects of report cards in the health industry has found mixed results. In one study, consumers were found to base their choice of HMO more on the subjective ratings reported on the cards (which are obtained from consumers themselves and are influenced by factors such as the comfort of waiting rooms and availability of parking) than on objective data (such as mammography rates and other data indicating conformance with best practices).[2] Similar phenomena seem to apply to consumer choice of software, which may be guided more by superficial convenience factors than by inherent quality. This is not to deny consumers the right to weigh factors as they please in their selection of products, of course, but it does mean that popularity with consumers should not be taken as prima facie evidence of quality.

ACCOUNTABILITY AND LIABILITY

Where there is a need to deploy certifiably dependable software, it should always be explicit who is accountable, professionally and legally, for any failure to achieve the declared dependability. One benefit of making dependability claims explicit is that accountability becomes possible; without explicit claims, there cannot even be a clear determination of what constitutes failure. Such accountability can be made explicit in the

---

[2]Dafny Leemore and David Dranove, 2005, "Do report cards tell consumers anything they don't already know? The case of Medicare HMOs," National Bureau of Economic Research Working Paper No. 11420, June.

purchase contract, as part of the certification of the software, as part of a professional licensing scheme, or in other ways. However, these are not true alternatives to one another because they interact—for example, a certification scheme might require the use of licensed staff as lead developers or as certifiers. No single solution will meet all the circumstances in which certifiably dependable software will be deployed, and accountability regimes should therefore be tailored to suit particular circumstances.

At present, it is common for software developers to disclaim, so far as possible, liability for defects in their products to a greater extent than customers and society expect from manufacturers in other industries. Clearly, no software should be considered dependable if it is supplied with a disclaimer that releases the manufacturer from providing a warranty or other remedies for software that fails to meet its dependability claims. Determining appropriate remedies, however, was beyond the scope of this study and would have required careful analysis of benefits and costs, taking into account not only the legal issues but also the state of software engineering, the various submarkets for software, economic impact, and the effect on innovation.

CERTIFICATION

To establish that software is dependable involves inspection and analysis of the dependability claim and the evidence that is offered in its support. Where the customers of the software are not able to carry out that work themselves (for lack of time or expertise) they will need to involve a third party whose judgment they can rely on to be independent of pressures from the vendor or other parties. Evaluating the dependability case is where certification regimes come into play.

Such independence must be demonstrated if third parties are to be successfully used in this role. Third-party assessors have been successful in other fields—the licensed engineers who carry out certificate-of-airworthiness inspections on aircraft, for example, and the "authorized bodies" who perform inspections in the European rail industry—and there is no fundamental reason that such assessment should not work in the software industry too.

Certification can take many forms, from self-certification to independent third-party certification by a licensed certification authority. No single certification regime is suitable for all circumstances, so a suitable scheme should be chosen by each customer and vendor to suit the circumstances of the particular requirement for certifiably dependable software. Industry groups and professional societies should consider developing model certification schemes for their industries, taking account of the detailed recommendations in this report. Any certification regime focusing on dependability should make use of a dependability case, as has been described throughout this report.

Certification should always explicitly allocate accountability for the failure of the software to meet the claimed dependability requirements. In general, such accountability should lie with the person making the claim for dependability—perhaps the software manufacturer, the system manufacturer (especially where COTS software has been incorporated in a system), or the certifier.

EVIDENCE AND OPENNESS

Evidence is the central theme of this report. In the arena of particular software products and systems, the committee has argued that confidence in the dependability of a system must rest on concrete evidence. And in the broader arena of technology advances, including finding better approaches and methodologies to developing software as well as developing innovative new tools, it has argued that evidence supporting or contradicting particular approaches is an essential enabler of progress. Determining whether to build and field a software system that could offer great benefits but also pose a potentially catastrophic risk calls for a plausible and transparent cost-benefit analysis that explicitly and carefully considers the evidence.

In both arenas—individual software products and technology advances—there is currently a dearth of evidence, which seriously hampered the committee's work, making it hard to resolve debate or reach an informed consensus on some issues. Obtaining and recording better evidence is crucial. A key obstacle is a lack of transparency and the inability to look into the system under consideration and see how it was developed. In some cases, evidence is not available. Many software developers, for example, are not withholding data but have simply not seriously considered using the evidence they have for evaluating the dependability of their product. In other cases, however, evidence exists but cannot be used effectively because no one who sees it has sufficient expertise.

Some software producers might be driven to hide evidence that could damage perceptions of their product. But others choose not to disclose evidence because they are reasonably concerned about revealing proprietary information that would aid competitors or because they have no incentive to pay the costs of organizing and disseminating the data. The committee is loath, therefore, to propose regulations or standards that might compel software producers to reveal proprietary information.

However, because such evidence would be valuable for the software industry and its consumers, it is important to rescue it from the shadows and make it more available. The committee encourages consumers to demand better information about the dependability of software products and to be suspicious of any dependability claims that are not allowed to be evaluated by an independent third party.

Likewise, the committee encourages those in government who procure and field critical systems to be skeptical of manufacturers' claims and to recognize that public scrutiny can be a good thing. In some domains, secrecy will remain important; it would not be sensible, for example, to insist that the designs and dependability cases for defense systems be made public. Secrecy, however, is often overrated, and much of the research community has come to believe that secrecy prevents it from examining the mechanism in question, robbing society of the peer review that would otherwise take place. Furthermore, the confidence of the public might be seriously undermined if important information is withheld by government officials that might bear on the decision to field a system. Electronic voting is a prime example of this. Despite accusations of serious failures and vulnerabilities in voting software, its manufacturers, along with the state officials who award the contracts and are responsible for assessing the dependability of the software, have in some cases been reluctant to give out information that would allow independent experts to make their own judgments and may have forfeited society's chance to have better software and may even have damaged the credibility of the electoral process itself.[3]

SECURITY CONCERNS

Because the committee has argued that the same broad principles should apply to a variety of systems in different application domains, it has not made recommendations specific to any particular area. Security, however, demands special consideration, because although security concerns are greater for certain kinds of systems, almost all systems are vulnerable to malicious attack to some degree. Effort invested in building a dependability case for a system is much less useful if there are security vulnerabilities that bring into question the most basic assumptions made about the behavior of components and their independence. In short, security vulnerabilities can undermine the entire dependability case and therefore need to be addressed as an integral part of the case.

Most software systems are networked and therefore open to attack;

---

[3]See, for example, National Research Council (NRC), 2006, "Letter report on electronic voting," The National Academies Press, Washington, D.C.; and NRC, 2005, *Asking the Right Questions About Electronic Voting*, The National Academies Press, Washington, D.C. Available online at <http://books.nap.edu/catalog.php?record_id=11704> and <http://books.nap.edu/catalog.php?record_id=11449>, respectively.

these clearly need a security audit. For systems that have been isolated, an audit is also likely to be essential, because the inconvenience of isolation is usually a response to the perceived risk of malicious attack.

The security of a product or system (and, consequently, certification thereof) involves two somewhat distinct facets of the product or system: (1) the presence of security features such as access controls that allow the owner of the product or system to define and enforce security policy and (2) the ability of the product or system to resist hostile attack.[4] However, it should also be noted that the mere presence of security features is not sufficient in and of itself. Indeed, given the increasing complexity of systems and security features, the usability and complexity of security configuration is a significant concern as well. It is important that it be likely, not just possible, that a system's administrators will configure its security features correctly. Due effort is needed to evaluate and show that feasible and expected configurations do not result in obvious vulnerabilities and to ensure that it is clear to those configuring the system what the appropriate configurations are.

The presence and correctness of security features can be certified by measures similar to those used to certify that other functional requirements are present and correct, and such certification is the domain of today's Common Criteria (CC). However, certification of the ability to resist attack needs to begin by considering the kinds of attacks that might be directed at the product or system (sometimes referred to as a threat analysis) and then proceeding to review the measures that the developer took to prevent attacks from being successful. This review examines not only the developer's process but also the effectiveness of the specific techniques that were applied to identify and remove vulnerabilities, and it rests on evidence that the developer in fact applied those techniques thoroughly and effectively.

While the CC assess security features, a new paradigm is needed to provide the owners of products and systems with a meaningful certification of resistance to attack. The approach to dependable software that this report proposes is germane to the development of such a certification paradigm. In particular, attention must be paid to articulating and evaluating assumptions about the environment in which the system operates and in which malicious attackers reside. The analysis is harder for security than for other properties, because the interface between the system and the environment is not easily described. This is true in general, of course. A system that controls a motor, for example, might need to account not

---

[4]For a brief overview of cybersecurity issues generally, see NRC, 2002, *Cybersecurity Today and Tomorrow: Pay Now or Pay Later*, The National Academies Press, Washington, D.C. Available online at <http://www.nap.edu/catalog.php?record_id=10274>.

only for the electrical load but also for the heating effect of the motor on nearby sensors. In the security realm, however, the concerns are central, since attackers aim to exploit hidden aspects of the interface that a security audit might have neglected. For example, attacks on smartcards, have been devised that rely on monitoring fluctuations in the electrical load that the device presents.[5] This means that security analysts should always be attentive to the risks of new kinds of attacks, and that security cases should be revisited as new attacks are discovered.

A REPOSITORY OF SOFTWARE DEPENDABILITY DATA

Transparency and openness alone are not enough, however. Few people have the time and expertise to carefully examine and understand arcane data. Developing a substantial repository of credible evidence will require a concerted effort to record, analyze and organize data. Such an effort would probably involve at least two distinct components, both aimed at involving software engineering experts more directly in accident analysis and reporting.

First, software experts should be actively involved in accident analysis. In many accidents software is either a contributing or a central factor, yet it is common for review panels not to examine the software at a level of detail commensurate with its role. Experts in other fields tend to minimize the role of software and underestimate the threats it poses. It is common, for example, to blame users for taking inappropriate actions despite egregious flaws in the design of the user interface.[6]

Second, reports of failures and accidents should, whenever possible, be accompanied by the software artifacts themselves so that experts can evaluate a report on the basis of the same evidence that was made available to the report's authors. Concerns about proprietary material and the risk of exposing security vulnerabilities in existing systems should of course be taken into account, but the ease of publishing large artifacts in the era of the Web and the value of making the information widely avail-

---

[5]See, for example, O. Kommerling and M. Kuhn, 1999, "Design principles for tamper-resistant smartcard processors," *Proceedings of the USENIX Workshop on Smartcard Technology (Smartcard '99)*, Chicago, Ill., May 10-11, USENIX Association, pp. 9-20. Available online at <http://www.cl.cam.ac.uk/~mgk25/sc99-tamper.pdf> for a discussion of various smartcard vulnerabilities.

[6]The Panama radiotherapy accidents are a good example of this phenomenon. See IAEA, 2001, "Investigation of an accidental exposure of radiotherapy patients in Panama: Report of a team of experts, 26 May-1 June 2001," IAEA, Vienna, Austria. Available online at <http://www-pub.iaea.org/MTCD/publications/PDF/Pub1114_scr.pdf>. Also, see M.H. Lützhöft and S.W.A. Dekker, 2002, "On your watch: Automation on the bridge," *Journal of Navigation* 55(1):83-96.

able should make disclosure the default position and place the burden of proof on those who would argue against it.

How exactly these goals should be achieved in terms of policy prescriptions is beyond the purview of this report. A centralized approach, in which government agencies (the FDA, NTSB, FAA, and so on) maintain public databases and supervise the collection and dissemination of data, might make certain aspects of this process, such as cross-comparisons, easier. On the other hand, there is value in decentralized approaches, in which software specialists form local teams that oversee software in particular domains and locations, such as the software oversight committees proposed by Gardner and Miller for medical software systems.[7]

EDUCATION

In many high school and indeed some college-level programming courses, students are introduced to programming as a mechanistic activity, in which programs are developed by trial and error. Such experimentation and exploration can be healthy; as in other fields of design and engineering, exploring new ideas is essential, especially for novices. However, as argued elsewhere in this report, the development of dependable software should ultimately be seen as an engineering activity—as argued elsewhere in this report. Thus a curricular emphasis on finding the essence of a program and solving it convincingly is preferable to mastering the accidental intricacies of particular software systems. Moreover, the absence of exemplars and overexposure to software that is overly complicated or otherwise poorly designed can make it harder to teach students to appreciate the important qualities of good design, such as clarity, simplicity, and fitness to purpose. Introducing the notion of dependability in educational contexts would require (1) a recognition of the real-world factors that lead to complexity and (2) discussion of explicit examples of clarity and simplicity in the design of large systems and the trade-offs involved in their design.

In high school computer science education, giving students a foundation in the ideas of dependability would require greater emphasis on programming as a design activity, on the qualities of a good program, and on the process of constructing programs and reasoning about them. The intricacies of the programming language or platform low-level execution details would receive less emphasis. Programming with an eye toward dependability and a rudimentary dependability case would be used to

---

[7]Randolph Miller and Reed M. Gardner, 1997, "Recommendations for responsible monitoring and regulation of clinical software systems," *Journal of the American Medical Informatics Association* (4):442-457.

help develop a student's ability to crystallize ideas and make them precise and to structure and dissect arguments.

Decisions on the curriculum are often motivated by the desire to make students "computer literate." The goal is laudable, but it is important that such literacy not be construed merely as familiarity with the details of today's software products. The ability to operate a computer and use standard desktop applications with basic competency is essential, but it is also important for students to have an understanding of how the computing infrastructure as a whole works and why it sometimes fails.[8] Computer literacy should not be confused with computer science and software engineering, and it is important that students understand the difference. In addition, mathematics is important for the education of software engineers, especially combinatorics and discrete mathematics, including the theory of sets, relations, and graphs.

At the university level, an emphasis on dependability would mean that the software and computer science curriculum should address more explicitly the topics that are the foundation for dependable software. Students need to have a broader understanding of the role of software and computers in larger systems and need to be familiar with the basic principles of systems engineering. Topics that support dependability include a basic introduction to formal methods, with an emphasis on system modeling rather than proofs of correctness, along with usability and human factors. Security and dependability are usually treated as specialized topics, but they should be integrated into the curriculum more fully and encountered by students repeatedly, especially when learning how to program.

The mathematical background of students studying computer science and software engineering would need to be expanded to include not only discrete mathematics (set theory and logic) but also probability and statistics, whose importance in many fields of computing is growing and which are particularly important for understanding dependability issues. Because the mathematics courses offered to computer science students are often designed with mathematicians in mind rather than engineers, they tend to focus on meta results and proof. Most computer science students, especially those interested in software, would benefit more from mathematics courses that focus on using mathematical constructs to model and reason about systems.

---

[8]For more on the importance of literacy and fluency with information technology, see the NRC report *Being Fluent with Information Technology* (National Academy Press, 1999, pp. 3-4), which argued that IT fluency "is fundamentally integrative, calling upon an individual to coordinate information and skills with respect to multiple dimensions of a problem and to make overall judgments and decisions taking all such information into account."

In software projects, one way to encourage attention to dependability concerns would be to require students to build programs that respond gracefully to unanticipated input as a way of introducing them to the most fundamental principles of building secure software. More generally, students should be encouraged not merely to achieve a running program that passes a suite of tests but also to develop a deeper understanding of why the program works and to assess their confidence in its dependability by developing minidependability cases of their own based on an honest appraisal of their own abilities, on the strength of their argument that it works, and on the significance and likelihood of adverse events in the environment.

RESEARCH

Although the committee believes that the approach outlined in this report might substantially improve the dependability of software, it recognizes that these measures alone cannot overcome the ever-growing demands for software with more complex functionality, operating in more invasive and critical contexts. Major technological advances are therefore essential for the future of the industry. While such advances might be produced by the computer industry alone, its history to date (and the dramatic success of federal investment, for example, in networking) suggests that advances will come more quickly and at lower cost if significant investments are made in fundamental research. In the United States, the High Confidence Software and Systems Coordinating Group (HCSS CG) of the National Coordination Office for Networking and Information Technology Research and Development (NITRD) coordinates many research activities in areas relevant to this report, focusing on

> scientific foundations and technologies for innovative systems design, systems and embedded application software, and assurance and verification to enable the routine production of reliable, robust, safe, scalable, secure, stable, and certifiably dependable IT-centric physical and engineered systems comprising new classes of advanced services and applications. These systems, often embedded in larger physical and IT systems, are essential for the operation of the country's critical societal infrastructures, acceleration of U.S. capability in industrial competitiveness, and optimization of citizens' quality of life.[9]

The importance of software dependability suggests that funding could be focused on areas that might lead to more dependable software.

---

[9]For more information, see the NITRD HCSS CG home page online at <http://www.nitrd.gov/subcommittee/hcss.html>.

Some areas that seem to merit attention and follow from the overarching recommendations and approach of this study are covered briefly below. They should not be construed as exclusive but as providing an indication of what sorts of research questions the approach raises:

- *Testing as evidence.* Testing is currently the most widely used technique for finding bugs in code, and when it is performed systematically and extensively, it can be an important element of a dependability case. As noted earlier in the report, however, it is hard to determine what level of dependability is assured when a system passes a given test suite. Clearly, an exhaustive test that covers every state and history that could possibly occur in the field would be tantamount to proof (and perhaps better). At the other end of the spectrum, passing a few dozen ad hoc tests provides little information about the flaws that might remain. The former approach is almost never feasible and the latter is insufficient. The gray area in the middle merits consideration. Can concrete dependability claims be based on limited testing? Can the absence of certain classes of error be assured by the successful execution of certain test cases? Could stronger claims be based on testing if novel forms of coverage (such as execution of all possible traces for a limited heap size or number of context switches) are used? Might testing with respect to a known operational profile be substantiated by online monitoring to ensure that the profile used for testing remains an accurate representation of actual operation? Although considerable literature on testing exists, there is an opportunity for further research to be undertaken focused specifically on methods that create evidence that a system has some explicit dependability properties to a high degree of confidence.
- *Checking code against domain-specific properties.* Recent years have seen many advances in techniques for automatic code checking, and there is renewed interest in program verification (witness the recent proposal of a Grand Challenge in this area[10]). These techniques will be essential to the construction of dependability cases, especially if they are capable of handling domain-specific properties rather than just local properties of the code that cannot be assembled into a systemwide argument for dependability.
- *Strong languages and tools for independence arguments.* As discussed above, the cost of constructing a case for dependability with respect to a particular critical property would be reduced by restricting the code-level argument to a small proportion of the modules. Using unsafe languages compromises any modularity that would otherwise make such an inde-

---

[10]See C.A.R. Hoare, 2003, "The verifying compiler: A grand challenge for computing research," *Journal of the ACM* 50(1):63-69.

pendence argument plausible. For example, as noted previously, in a program written in a language such as C, an out-of-bounds array access can overwrite data structures that are not accessible by name, so that one cannot rely on the use of names to determine how one module might interact with another. Research is needed to understand whether using safe languages or other tools could justify independence and help structure dependability arguments, and how independence arguments might be made when there are good reasons to use an unsafe language.

• *Composing component dependability cases.* Complex software components are seldom furnished with the information needed to support dependability arguments for the systems that use them. For use within a larger argument, the details of the dependability case of a component need not be known. Until recently, there has been little demand for components to be delivered with the claims, arguments, and evidence needed to support the dependability case for a system that uses the component. At lower levels of criticality, and in accidental systems, explicit dependability cases have seldom been constructed, so there has been no perceived need for component-level cases. At the other extreme, the dependability cases for systems with highly critical assurance goals (such as airplanes) have focused on the details of their components. In addition, there have been few regulatory mechanisms applicable to such systems to support the use of prequalified critical components that would allow the dependability case for the larger system to use the applicable cases for its components without inquiring into all the details of the components themselves. With greater reuse of components, and a concomitant awareness of the risks involved (especially of using commodity operating systems in critical settings), component-level assurance will become an essential activity throughout the industry, and it will be necessary to find ways to compose the dependability arguments of components into an argument for the system as a whole. The research challenges involve not only investigating how this might be done, but also how to account for, and mitigate, varying levels of confidence in the component arguments.

• *Modeling and reasoning about environments.* As explained earlier in this report, the dependability of a system usually rests on assumptions about the behavior of operators and devices in the environment of the system and, more broadly, on the human organization in which the system is deployed. The dependability case should therefore involve reasoning about interactions between the system and its environment. The necessary formal foundations for such reasoning are perhaps already available, since an operator or physical device can be modeled along with the system, for example, as a state machine. It is not clear, however, how to model the environment and structure environmental assumptions; how to account for human behavior or larger organizational effects; how to handle normal and malicious users; or how to express crucial properties.

• *Reasoning about fail-stop systems.* The critical dependability properties of most critical systems will take the form "X should never happen, but if it does, then Y must happen." For example, the essential property of a radiotherapy machine is that it not overdose the patient. Yet some amount of overdose occurs in many systems, and any overdose that occurs must be reported. Similarly, any fail-stop system is built in the hope that certain failures will never occur but is designed to fail in a safe way should they occur. It therefore seems likely that multiple dependability cases are needed, at different levels of assurance, each making different assumptions about which adverse events in the environment and failures in the system itself might occur. The structuring of these cases and their relationship to one another is an important topic of investigation.

• *Making stronger arguments from weaker ones.* A chain can be stronger than even its strongest link if the links are joined in parallel rather than in series. Similarly, weaker arguments can be combined to form a single stronger argument. A dependability case will typically involve evidence of different sorts, each contributing some degree of confidence to the overall dependability claim. It would be valuable to investigate such combinations, to determine what additional credibility each argument brings, and under what conditions of independence such credibility can be maximized.

4

Findings and Recommendations

In this chapter, the committee distills its proposed approach and findings and briefly discusses its recommendations for achieving justifiable confidence in dependable software systems.

FINDINGS

Improvements in software development are needed to keep pace with societal demands for software. Avoidable software failures have already been responsible for loss of life and for large economic losses. The quality of software produced by the industry is extremely variable, and there is inadequate oversight in some critical areas. Unless improvements are made, more pervasive deployment of software in the civic infrastructure[1] may lead to catastrophic failures. Software has the potential to bring dramatic benefits to society, but it will not be possible to realize these benefits—especially in critical applications—unless software becomes more dependable.

More data are needed about software failures and the efficacy of development approaches. Assessment of the state of the software industry, the risks posed by software, and progress made is currently hampered

---

[1]As an indication of the growth in the pervasiveness of software, the Bureau of Labor Statistics found in 2003 that the output of prepackaged software increased annually by 26.5 percent between 1990 and 2000, growth attributed to "the increased use of computers and the rising demand for reliable, user-friendly software." See <http://www.bls.gov/opub/ted/2003/feb/wk3/art01.htm>.

by the lack of a coherent source of information about software failures. Careful documentation and analysis of failures has had dramatic impact in other areas. More attention should be paid to the contributions of software to accidents, and repositories of accident reports are needed that include sufficient details to enable the analysis of trends and an evaluation of technologies and methods. Without a concerted effort to collect better data, investment in software technology and research may be misdirected, ineffective practices will remain, and adoption of the most effective methods will be hindered. In the absence of a federal initiative, the situation might improve dramatically if all the parties currently involved in software production, regulation, and accident reporting were to monitor systems more pervasively and systematically for failures; involve software experts to a greater degree in the investigation of failures of systems that include software as a component; and insist on greater transparency in every aspect of software development and deployment than is currently expected.

RECOMMENDATIONS

To Builders and Users of Software

Make the most of effective software development technologies and formal methods. A variety of modern technologies—in particular, safe programming languages, static analysis, and formal methods—are likely to reduce the cost and difficulty of producing dependable software. Elementary best practices, such as source code control and systematic defect tracking, should be universally adopted, and development organizations that fail to use them should not be regarded as sources of dependable software. Advanced practitioners, especially those working in specialized domains, may be justified in creating their own framework of processes and practices that embodies these recommended elements. But those who are not already familiar with the best practices of the industry (described previously) should first ensure that their developments adhere to these elements and then consider diverging only under extraordinary circumstances. Formal methods have been shown to be effective only for small to medium-sized critical systems and have not been widely adopted. Furthermore, they require a new mindset and may demand staff with greater expertise, especially in the early stages of development. Nevertheless, key elements of formal techniques would aid in the cost-effective construction of dependability cases and could be widely applied, especially in combination with the incrementality and minimality encouraged in some development approaches such as those currently labeled "agile."

Follow proven principles for software development. The committee's proposed approach also includes adherence to the following principles:

- *Take a systems perspective.* A systems perspective should be adopted in which the dependability of software is viewed not in terms of intrinsic properties (such as the incidence of bugs in the code) but in terms of the system as a whole, including interactions among people, process, and technology and encompassing both the physical and organizational environment of the system. Engineering of software should be driven by a consideration of risks and their mitigation, and well-established risk analysis and reduction techniques that are applied in other domains (such as hazard analysis) should be routinely applied to software. Different levels of assurance will be appropriate for different systems and for dependability properties within a single system.
- *Exploit simplicity.* If dependability is to be achieved at reasonable cost, simplicity should become a key goal, and developers and customers must be willing to accept the compromises it entails. Unfettered growth in the complexity of the functionality offered is incompatible with dependability. The architecture of the software should reflect the prioritization of requirements, ideally so that the critical properties can be established by examining closely only a small portion of the software, relying on independence arguments to account for lack of interference from the remaining portions.

Make a dependability case for a given system and context: evidence, explicitness, and expertise. A software system should be regarded as dependable only if sufficient evidence is presented to substantiate the dependability claim. The evidence should take the form of a dependability case that explains why the critical properties hold, and it will involve reasoning about both the code and the environmental assumptions. To the extent that this reasoning can be supported by automated tools, it will be more credible. The dependability properties should be explicitly articulated and carefully prioritized; the assumed properties of the environment should be made explicit also. This approach gives considerable leeway to developers to use whatever practices are best suited to the problem at hand. In particular, it allows the use of less robust components and languages at the expense of having to mitigate the risk with a more elaborate dependability argument. Despite this flexibility, in practice the challenges of developing dependable software are sufficiently great that developers will need considerable expertise and will have to justify any deviations from best practices.

Demand more transparency, so that customers and users can make more informed judgments about dependability. Customers and users can make informed judgments when choosing suppliers and products only if the claims, criteria, and evidence for dependability are transparent. The willingness of a supplier to provide data beyond the dependability case proper (about the qualifications of personnel, its track record in providing dependable software, and the process it used) and the clarity and integrity of the data that it provides will be a strong indicator of its attitude toward dependability.

Make use of but do not rely solely on process and testing. Testing will be an essential component of a dependability case but will not in general suffice, because even the largest test suites typically used will not exercise enough paths to provide evidence that the software is correct, nor will they have sufficient statistical significance for the levels of confidence usually desired. Testing is a vital aspect of every development, not only because it exposes flaws but also because it provides feedback on the quality of the development process. Software that fails many test cases probably cannot be made dependable and should perhaps be abandoned. Adherence to a particular process will not suffice as evidence either. There is no established universal correlation between process and dependability, although demonstrated adherence to process contributes to the dependability case. In other words, rigorous process is essential for preserving the chain of dependability evidence but is not per se evidence of dependability. Without a rigorous process, however, evidence produced by the developers will not be credible, and it is unlikely that the developing organization will be able to identify and correct flaws in the way it produces software. An effective process need not be a burdensome one, and too elaborate a process (especially if it requires the production of excessive documentation) can be damaging.

Base certification on inspection and analysis of the dependability claim and the evidence offered in its support. Because testing and process alone are insufficient, the dependability claim will require, in addition, evidence produced by analysis. Analysis may involve well-reasoned informal argument, formal proofs of code correctness, and mechanical inference (as performed, for example, by type checkers). Indeed, the dependability case for even a relatively simple system will usually require all of these kinds of analysis, and they will need to be fitted together into a coherent whole. A developer that uses COTS components will either have to demonstrate in the dependability case that their failure will not undermine the crucial dependability properties or will have to incorporate in the case appropriate claims about the properties of the components themselves. Absent careful engineering, a system can become as vulnerable as its weakest components, so the inclusion of standard desktop software in critical applications should be carefully examined. Where the customer for the software is not able to carry out that work itself (through lack of time or lack of expertise) it will need to involve a third party whose judgment it can rely on to be independent of commercial pressures from the vendor. Certification can take many forms, from self-certification through independent third-party certification by a licensed certification authority.

Include security considerations in the dependability case. By violating assumptions about how components behave, about their interactions, or about the expected behavior of users, security vulnerabilities can undermine the case made for dependability properties. The dependability case must therefore account explicitly for security risks that might compromise its other aspects. It is also important to ensure that security certifications give meaningful assurance of resistance to attack. Owners of products and systems whose security has been certified expect that if they deploy the products and systems properly, most attacks against those products or systems will fail. Today's security certification regimes do not provide this confidence, and new security certification regimes are needed. Such certification regimes can be built by applying the other findings and recommendations of this report, with an emphasis on the role of the environment—in particular, the assumptions made about the potential actions of a hostile attacker and the likelihood that new classes of vulnerabilities will be discovered and new attacks developed to exploit them.

Demand accountability and make it explicit. Where there is a need to deploy certifiably dependable software, it should always be made explicit who is accountable, professionally and legally, for any failure to achieve the declared dependability. At present, it is common for software developers to disclaim liability for defects in their products to a greater extent than customers and society expect from manufacturers in other industries. Clearly, no software should be considered dependable if it is supplied with a disclaimer that withholds the manufacturer's commitment to provide a warranty or other remedies for software that fails to meet its dependability claims. The appropriate scope of remedies was not determined in this study, however, and would require a careful analysis of benefits and costs.

To Agencies and Organizations That Support
Software Education and Research

The committee was not constituted or charged to recommend budget levels or to assess trade-offs between software dependability and other priorities. However, the committee does conclude that the increasing importance of software to society and the extraordinary challenge currently faced in producing software of adequate dependability provide a strong rationale for investment in education and research initiatives.

Place greater emphasis on dependability—and its fundamental underpinnings—in the high school, undergraduate, and graduate education of software developers. Many practitioners do not have an adequate appreciation of software dependability issues, are not aware of the most effective development practices, or are not capable of applying them appropriately. A focus on dependability considerations in high school, undergraduate, and graduate educational contexts is therefore needed. The importance of dependability for software is not adequately stressed in most degree programs in the United States. More emphasis should be placed on systems thinking; on requirements, specification, and large-scale design; on security; on usability; on the development of robust and resilient code; on basic discrete mathematics and statistics; and on the construction and analysis of dependability arguments.

Federal agencies that support information technology research and development should give priority to basic research to further software-enabled system dependability, emphasizing a systems perspective and evidence. Until there is a dramatic improvement in the methods, languages, and tools of software development, there will be systems that cannot be constructed to appropriate levels of dependability. Moreover, even when this is possible, the cost will be higher than it should be. Because of the increasing importance of software to our society and the extraordinary challenge of producing software of adequate dependability, research is needed that emphasizes a systems perspective and "the three E's," and such research should be a priority for funding agencies. The research should be informed by a systems view that assigns greater value to advances that are likely to have an impact in a world of large systems interacting with other systems and operators in a complex physical environment and organizational context.

* * *

The committee believes that the approach discussed here will substantially improve the dependability of many critical software systems being produced today. While the economic trade-offs are different in individual cases, the committee believes that its recommendations are generally applicable to many non-safety-critical systems as well—a consideration that becomes increasingly important as COTS components are reused in critical systems and accidental systems are formed from a mix of critical and noncritical components. Applying the committee's approach to all software systems, safety-critical and non-safety-critical alike, promises to alleviate the heavy costs and frustrations that low-quality software imposes even in noncritical applications.

In the long term, innovations in software engineering are likely to bring dramatic improvements in dependability. Software systems are complex and, just as in other sorts of complex systems, failures will inevitably occur. But if our society succeeds in this ambitious program, we can hope that, 10 or 20 years from now, the adoption of ambitious and potentially dangerous new systems will be justified by rational arguments; a broad consensus in the software industry will guide standard practice; the production of software will be less expensive and more predictable than it is today; and the incidence of software failures will be low and well-documented.

5

Bibliography

Adams, E. 1984. "Optimizing Preventive Service of Software Products." *IBM Journal of Research* 28(1):2-14.

Akerlof, George A. 1970. "The Market for 'Lemons': Quality Uncertainty and the Market Mechanism." *Quarterly Journal of Economics* 84(3):488-500.

Alves-Foss, Jim, Bob Rinker, and Carol Taylor. 2002. "Merging Safety and Assurance: The Process of Dual Certification for FAA and the Common Criteria." Available online at <http://www.csds.uidaho.edu/comparison/slides.pdf>.

Amey, Peter. 2002. "Correctness by Construction: Better Can Also Be Cheaper," *Cross-Talk Magazine, The Journal of Defence Software Engineering*, March. Available online at <http://www.praxis-his.com/pdfs/c_by_c_better_cheaper.pdf>.

Avizienis, A., J.-C. Laprie, B. Randell, and C. Landwehr. 2004. "Basic Concepts and Taxonomy of Dependable and Secure Computing." *IEEE Transactions on Dependable and Secure Computing* 1(1):11-33.

Barnes, John. 2003. *High Integrity Software: The SPARK Approach to Safety and Security*. Addison-Wesley, Boston, Mass.

BBC News. 2005. "Hospital Struck by Computer Virus." August 22. Available online at <http://news.bbc.co.uk/1/hi/england/merseyside/4174204.stm>.

Beck, Kent. 1999. *Extreme Programming Explained: Embrace Change*. Addison-Wesley, New York.

Besnard, D., C. Gacek, and C.B. Jones, eds. 2006. *Structure for Dependability*, Springer-Verlag, New York.

Boyapati, Chandrasekhar, Sarfraz Khurshid, and Darko Marinov. 2002. "Korat: Automated Testing Based on Java Predicates." *ACM/SIGSOFT International Symposium on Software Testing and Analysis*, Rome, Italy. July.

Butler, R., and G. Finelli. 1993. "The Infeasibility of Quantifying the Reliability of Life-Critical Real-Time Software." *IEEE Transactions on Software Engineering* 19(1):3-12.

Chapman, R., and A. Hall. 2002. "Correctness by Construction: Developing a Commercially Secure System." *IEEE Software* (January/February):18-25.

Chillarege, R. 1999. "Software Testing Best Practices," IBM Technical Report RC 21457 Log 96856.

Civil Aviation Authority. 2003. "CAP 670: Air Traffic Services Safety Requirements." Available online at <http://www.caa.co.uk/docs/33/cap670.pdf>.

Computer Economics. 2003. "Virus Attack Costs on the Rise—Again." Available online at <http://www.computereconomics.com/article.cfm?id=873>.

Cook, Richard, and Michael O'Connor. Forthcoming. "Thinking About Accidents and Systems," in Improving Medication Safety, K. Thompson and H. Manasse, eds. American Society of Health-System Pharmacists, Washington, D.C.

Cook, R., and J. Rasmussen. 2005. "Going Solid: A Model of System Dynamics and Consequences for Patient Safety." Quality and Safety in Health Care 14(2):130-134.

Cook, R.I., D.D. Woods, and M.B. Howie. 1992. "Unintentional Delivery of Vasoactive Drugs with an Electromechanical Infusion Device." Journal of Cardiothoracic and Vascular Anesthesia 6:238-244.

Cook, R.I., D.D. Woods, and C. Miller. 1998. "A Tale of Two Stories: Contrasting Views on Patient Safety." National Patient Safety Foundation, Chicago, Ill., April. Available online at <http://www.npsf.org/exec/report.html>.

Cusumano, Michael A., and David B. Yoffie. 1998. Competing on Internet Time: Lessons from Netscape and Its Battle with Microsoft. Free Press, New York.

Dahl, O.J., E.W. Dijkstra, and C.A.R. Hoare. 1972. Structured Programming. Academic Press, New York.

Department of Transportation, Office of the Inspector General. 2005. "Status of FAA's major acquisitions: Cost growth and schedule delays continue to stall air traffic modernization." Report Number AV-2005-061, May 26.

Dornheim, Michael A. 2005. "Codes gone awry." Aviation Week & Space Technology, February 28, p. 63.

FAA (Federal Aviation Administration). 2003. Charter for the Certification Process Study (CPS) Response Aviation Rulemaking Committee. January 16.

FAA. 2004. "Reusable Software Components" (AC 20-148). FAA, Washington, D.C. Available online at <http://www.airweb.faa.gov/Regulatory_and_Guidance_Library/rgAdvisoryCircular.nsf/0/FBFCCB29C0E78FFF86256F6300617BDD?OpenDocument>.

FDA (Food and Drug Administration). 2002. "General Principles of Software Validation; Final Guidance for Industry and FDA Staff." Available online at <http://www.fda.gov/cdrh/comp/guidance/938.html>.

FDA. 2003. "Why Is Human Factors Engineering Important for Medical Devices?" Available online at <http://www.fda.gov/cdrh/humanfactors/important.html>.

Fenton, N.E., and M. Neil. 1998. "A Strategy for Improving Safety Related Software Engineering Standards." IEEE Transactions on Software Engineering 24(11):1002-1013.

Fitzgibbon, Chris. 1998. "Impact of ISO 9001 on Software Quality." Capital Quality News. Available online at <http://www.orioncanada.com/Impact.htm>.

Frankl, Phyllis G., and Elaine J. Weyuker. 1993. "A Formal Analysis of the Fault-Detecting Ability of Testing Methods." IEEE Transactions on Software Engineering 19(3):202-213.

Freeman, Sholnn. 2005. "Toyota Attributes Prius Shutdowns to Software Glitch." Wall Street Journal, May 16. Available online at <http://online.wsj.com/article_print/SB111619464176634063.html>.

Gacek, Cristina, and Budi Arief. 2004. "The Many Meanings of Open Source." IEEE Software 21(1):34-40.

Gage, Deborah, and John McCormick. 2004. "We Did Nothing Wrong." Baseline, March 4. Available online at <http://www.baselinemag.com/article2/0,1540,1543571,00.asp>.

GAO (General Accounting Office). 1986. "Medical Devices: Early Warning of Problems Is Hampered by Severe Underreporting," U.S. Government Printing Office, Washington, D.C. GAO publication PEMD-87-1.

GAO. 1992. *Patriot Missile Software Problem*. Report of the Information Management and Technology Division. Available online at <http://www.fas.org/spp/starwars/gao/im92026.htm>.

GAO. 2003. "Tactical Aircraft, Status of the F/A-22 Program: Statement of Allen Li, Director, Acquisition and Sourcing Management." GAO-33-603T. April 2.

Gardner, Reed M., and Randolph Miller. 1997. "Recommendations for Responsible Monitoring and Regulation of Clinical Software Systems." *Annals of Internal Medicine* 127(9): 842-845.

Geppert, L. 2004. "Lost Radio Contact Leaves Pilots on Their Own," *IEEE Spectrum* 41(11):16-17, November.

German, Andy, and Gavin Mooney. 2001. "Air Vehicle Software Static Code Analysis—Lessons Learnt." *Proceedings of the Ninth Safety-Critical Systems Symposium*. Felix Redmill and Tom Anderson, eds. Springer-Verlag, Bristol, United Kingdom.

Glass, Robert L. 2005. "IT Failure Rates—70 Percent or 10-15 Percent?" *IEEE Software* 22(3):112.

Goetz, Brian, Tim Peierls, Joshua Bloch, Joseph Bowbeer, David Holmes, and Doug Lea. 2006. *Java Concurrency in Practice*. Addison-Wesley, Boston, Mass.

GPS News. 2004. "Tanker Truck Shutdown via Satellite." Available online at <http://www.spacedaily.com/news/gps-03zn.html>.

Greenwell, William S., and John C. Knight. 2005. "What Should Aviation Safety Incidents Teach Us?" Technical Report CS-2003-12. University of Virginia, Charlottesville, Va. Available online at <http://www.cs.virginia.edu/~techrep/CS-2003-12.pdf>.

Grimaldi, James V., and Guy Gugliotta. 2001. "Chemical Plants Feared as Targets." *Washington Post*, December 16, p. A01.

Guth, Robert. 2003. "Make Software More Reliable." *The Wall Street Journal*. November 17.

Guttman, William. 2002. "The Private Sector: Sustainable Computing." *Pittsburgh Post-Gazette*, December 10. Available online at <http://www.post-gazette.com/businessnews/20021210forumguttmanp6.asp>.

Hall, Anthony. 1996. "Using Formal Methods to Develop an ATC Information System." *IEEE Software* 13(2):66-76.

Hammond, J., R. Rawlings, and A. Hall. 2001. "Will It Work?" *Proceedings of the 5th IEEE International Symposium on Requirements Engineering*, August.

Hilton, Adrian. 2003. "Engineering Software Systems for Customer Acceptance." Available online at <http://www.praxis-his.co.uk/pdfs/customer_acceptance.pdf>.

Hinchey, Michael G., and Jonathan P. Bowen, eds. 1999. *Industrial-Strength Formal Methods in Practice*. Springer, London, United Kingdom.

Hoare, C.A.R. 1981. "The Emperor's Old Clothes" (Turing Award Lecture), *Communications of the ACM* 24(2):75-83. Available online at <http://portal.acm.org/citation.cfm?id=358561>.

Hoare, C.A.R. 1996. "How Did Software Get So Reliable Without Proof?" *Lecture Notes in Computer Science* 1051:1-17.

Hoare, C.A.R.. 2003. "The Verifying Compiler: A Grand Challenge for Computing Research." *Journal of the ACM* 50(1):63–69.

Hollnagel, E., D.D. Woods, and N. Leveson, eds. 2006. *Resilience Engineering: Concepts and Precepts*. Ashgate, Aldershot, United Kingdom.

Holzmann, G.J. 2006. "The Power of Ten: Rules for Developing Safety Critical Code." *IEEE Computer* 39(6):95-97.

IAEA (International Atomic Energy Agency). 2001. "Investigation of an Accidental Exposure of Radiotherapy Patients in Panama: Report of a Team of Experts, 26 May-1 June 2001." IAEA, Vienna, Austria. Available online at <http://www-pub.iaea.org/MTCD/publications/PDF/Pub1114_scr.pdf>.

Institute of Medicine. 2000. *To Err Is Human: Building a Safer Health System.* National Academy Press, Washington, D.C. Available online at <http://books.nap.edu/catalog. php?record_id=9728>.

Instrument Society of America. 1996. "Application of Safety Instrumented Systems for the Process Industries." ISA-S-84.01-1996 (S84.01).

Jackson, D., and J. Wing. 1996. "Lightweight Formal Methods." *IEEE Computer Magazine* 29(4)21-22.

Jackson, Michael. 1996. *Software Requirements & Specifications.* Addison-Wesley and ACM Press.

Jackson, Michael. 2000. "The Real World." In *Millennial Perspectives in Computer Science: Proceedings of the 1999 Oxford-Microsoft Symposium in Honour of C A R Hoare,* Jim Davies, Bill Roscoe, and Jim Woodcock, eds. Palgrave Macmillan.

Jackson, Michael. 2001. *Problem Frames: Analysing and Structuring Software Development Problems.* Addison-Wesley, Boston, Mass.

Jackson, Michael. 2004. "Seeing More of the World." *IEEE Software* 21(6):83-85. Available online at <http://mcs.open.ac.uk/mj665/SeeMore3.pdf>.

Johnson, C.W. 2003. *Failure in Safety-Critical Systems: A Handbook of Accident and Incident Reporting.* University of Glasgow Press, Glasgow, Scotland.

Keizer, Gregg. 2004. "Unprotected PCs fall to hacker bots in just four minutes." *Tech Web,* November 30. Available online at <http://www.techweb.com/wire/ security/54201306>.

Khurshid, S., and D. Marinov. 2004. "TestEra: Specification-based Testing of Java Programs Using SAT." *Automated Software Engineering Journal* 11(4):403-434.

Kilbridge, Peter. 2003. "Computer Crash: Lessons from a System Failure." *New England Journal of Medicine* 348(March 6):881-882.

King, S., J. Hammond, R. Chapman, and A. Pryor, eds. 2000. "Is Proof More Cost-Effective Than Testing?" *IEEE Transactions on Software Engineering* 26(8):675-686.

Knight, John C. 2002. "Software Challenges in Aviation Systems." *Lecture Notes in Computer Science* 2434:106-112.

Koppel, Ross, Joshua P. Metlay, Abigail Cohen, Brian Abaluck, A. Russell Localio, Stephen E. Kimmel, and Brian L. Strom. 2005. "Role of Computerized Physician Order Entry Systems in Facilitating Medication Errors." *Journal of the American Medical Association* 293(10):1197-1203.

Kommerling, O., and M. Kuhn. 1999. "Design Principles for Tamper-Resistant Smartcard Processors," *Proceedings of the USENIX Workshop on Smartcard Technology (Smartcard '99),* Chicago, Ill., May 10-11. USENIX Association. Available online at <http://www. cl.cam.ac.uk/~mgk25/sc99-tamper.pdf>

Ladkin, Peter, translator. 1994. Translation of *Report on the Accident to Airbus A320-211 Aircraft in Warsaw on 14 September 1993.* Main Commission, Aircraft Accident Investigation, Warsaw. Available online at <http://www.rvs.uni-bielefeld.de/publications/ Incidents/DOCS/ComAndRep/Warsaw/warsaw-report.html>.

Lampson, Butler. 1983. "Hints for Computer System Design." *ACM Operating Systems Review* 17(5):33-48. Reprinted in *IEEE Software* 1(1):11-28. Available online at <http://research. microsoft.com/lampson/33-Hints/WebPage.html>.

Layton, C., P.J. Smith, and C.E. McCoy. 1994. "Design of a Cooperative Problem-Solving System for En-route Flight Planning: An Empirical Evaluation." *Human Factors* 36:94-119.

Lee, Insup, and George Pappas. 2005. *Final Report of High Confidence Medical Device Software and Systems (HCMDSS) Workshop,* Philadelphia, Pa., June 2-3. Available online at <http://rtg.cis.upenn.edu/hcmdss/HCMDSS-final-report-060206.pdf>.

Leemore, Dafny, and David Dranove. 2005. "Do Report Cards Tell Consumers Anything They Don't Already Know? The Case of Medicare HMOs," NBER Working Paper No. 11420. National Bureau of Economic Research, Cambridge, Mass.

Leveson, Nancy. 1995. *Safeware: System Safety and Computers.* Addison-Wesley, Boston, Mass.

Leveson, Nancy, and Clark S. Turner. 1993. "An Investigation of the Therac-25 Accidents." *IEEE Computer* 26(7):18-41.

Levy, Matthys, and Mario Salvadori. 1992. *Why Buildings Fall Down.* W.W. Norton & Company, New York.

Lin, L., R. Isla, K. Doniz, H. Harkness, K. Vicente, and D. Doyle. 1998. "Applying Human Factors to the Design of Medical Equipment: Patient Controlled Analgesia." *Journal of Clinical Monitoring* 14:253-263.

Lin, L., K. Vicente, and D.J. Doyle. 2001. "Patient Safety, Potential Adverse Drug Events, and Medical Device Design: A Human Factors Engineering Approach." *Journal of Biomedical Informatics* 34(4):274-284.

Lions, J.L. 1996. "ARIANE 5: Flight 501 Failure." Report by the Inquiry Board. Available online at <http://www.cs.unibo.it/~laneve/papers/ariane5rep.html>.

Litchfield, David. 2006. "Which Database Is More Secure? Oracle vs. Microsoft." NGSSoftware Insight Security Research. Available online at <http://www.databasesecurity.com/dbsec/comparison.pdf>.

Littlewood, B., and L. Strigini. 1993. "Validation of Ultra-High Dependability for Software-Based Systems." *Communications of the ACM* 36(11):69-80.

Loeb, Vernon. 2002. "'Friendly Fire' Deaths Traced to Dead Battery: Taliban Targeted, but U.S. Forces Killed." *Washington Post*, March 24, p. A21.

Lohr, Steve. 2003. "2 Companies to Announce U.S. Clearance for Linux Security." *New York Times*, August 5. Available online at <http://www.nytimes.com/2003/08/05/technology/05BLUE.html>.

LynuxWorks. 2002. "LynuxWorks to Offer First DO-178B Certifiable POSIX RTOS." December 10. Available online at <http://www.lynuxworks.com/corporate/news/press/2002/121002a.php3>.

MacKenzie, Donald. 2001. *Mechanizing Proof: Computing, Risk, and Trust.* MIT Press, Cambridge, Mass.

Maisel, William H., Michael O. Sweeney, William G. Stevenson, Kristin E. Ellison, and Laurence M. Epstein. 2001. "Recalls and Safety Alerts Involving Pacemakers and Implantable Cardioverter-defibrillator Generators." *Journal of the American Medical Association* 286:793-799.

Michaels, Daniel, and Andy Pasztor. 2006. "Incidents Prompt New Scrutiny of Airplane Software Glitches." *Wall Street Journal*, May 30, p. A1.

Miller, Randolph, and Reed M. Gardner. 1997. "Recommendations for Responsible Monitoring and Regulation of Clinical Software Systems." *Journal of the American Medical Informatics Association* (4):442-457.

Montgomery, Kathryn. 2006. *How Doctors Think, Clinical Judgment and the Practice of Medicine.* Oxford University Press, Oxford, United Kingdom.

Naur, P., and B. Randell, eds. 1969. *Software Engineering: Report on a Conference Sponsored by the NATO Science Committee.* Garmisch, Germany, October 7-11. NATO Scientific Affairs Division, Brussels, Belgium. Available online at <http://homepages.cs.ncl.ac.uk/brian.randell/NATO/>.

Nebeker, Jonathan R., Jennifer M. Hoffman, Charlene R. Weir, Charles L. Bennett, and John F. Hurdle. 2005. "High Rates of Adverse Drug Events in a Highly Computerized Hospital." *Archives of Internal Medicine* 165:1111-1116.

NRC (National Research Council). 1999a. *Being Fluent with Information Technology.* National Academy Press, Washington, D.C. Available online at <http://books.nap.edu/catalog.php?record_id=6482>.

NRC. 1999b. *Trust in Cyberspace.* National Academy Press, Washington, D.C. Available online at <http://books.nap.edu/catalog.php?record_id=6161>.

NRC. 2002. *Cybersecurity Today and Tomorrow: Pay Now or Pay Later.* The National Academies Press, Washington, D.C. Available online at <http://www.nap.edu/catalog.php?record_id=10274>.

NRC. 2003a. *Critical Information Infrastructure Protection and the Law: An Overview of Key Issues.* The National Academies Press, Washington, D.C. Available online at <http://books.nap.edu/catalog.php?record_id=10274>.

NRC. 2003b. *The Internet Under Crisis Conditions: Learning from September 11.* The National Academies Press, Washington, D.C. Available online at <http://books.nap.edu/catalog.php?record_id=10685>.

NRC. 2004. *Summary of a Workshop on Software Certification and Dependability.* The National Academies Press, Washington, D.C. Available online at <http://books.nap.edu/catalog.php?record_id=10569>.

NRC. 2005. *Asking the Right Questions About Electronic Voting.* The National Academies Press, Washington, D.C. Available online at <http://www.nap.edu/catalog.php?record_id=11449>.

NRC. 2006. "Letter Report on Electronic Voting." The National Academies Press, Washington, D.C. Available online at <http://www.nap.edu/catalog.php?record_id=11704>.

Nunnally, M., C.P. Nemeth, V. Brunetti, and R.I. Cook. 2004. "Lost in Menuspace: User Interactions with Complex Medical Devices." *IEEE Transactions on Systems, Man and Cybernetics—Part A: Systems and Humans* 34(6):736-742.

Olavsrud, Thor. 2003. "White House E-mail System Slows to a Crawl." *Dc.internet.com*, July 18. Available online at <http://dc.internet.com/news/article.php/2237391>.

Page, D., P. Williams, and D. Boyd. 1993. *Report of the Inquiry into the London Ambulance Service*, Communications Directorate, South West Thames Regional Health Authority, London, February. Available online at <http://www.cs.ucl.ac.uk/staff/A.Finkelstein/las/lascase0.9.pdf>.

Parnas, D.L., and J. Madey. 1995. "Functional Documentation for Computer Systems." *Science of Computer Programming* 25(1):41-61.

Perlis, Alan J. 1982. "Epigrams on Programming." *SIGPLAN Notices* 17(9):7-13.

Perrow, Charles. 1999. *Normal Accidents.* Princeton University Press, Princeton, N.J.

Perrow, Charles. 2007. *The Next Catastrophe: Reducing Our Vulnerabilities to Natural, Industrial, and Terrorist Disasters.* Princeton University Press, Princeton, N.J.

Perry, Shawna J., Robert L. Wears, and Richard I. Cook. 2005. "The Role of Automation in Complex System Failures." *Journal of Patient Safety* 1(1):56-61.

Petroski, Henry. 2004. *To Engineer Is Human.* St Martin's Press, New York.

Pfleeger, Shari Lawrence. 1998. "Understanding and Improving Technology Transfer in Software Engineering." Report DACS-SOAR-98-1. DoD Data and Analysis Center for Software.

Pfleeger, Shari Lawrence, and Les Hatton. 1997. "Investigating the Influence of Formal Methods." *IEEE Computer* 30(2):33-43.

Research Triangle Institute. 2002. *The Economic Impacts of Inadequate Infrastructure for Software Testing* (Final Report). Prepared for Gregory Tassey, National Institute of Standards and Technology, Acquisition and Assistance Division. Available online at <http://www.rti.org/pubs/software_testing.pdf>.

Rice, Lynne L., and Andrew Lowery. 1995. "Premarket Notification 510(K): Regulatory Requirements for Medical Devices." Division of Small Manufacturers Assistance. U.S. Department of Health and Human Services, Publication FDA 95-4158. Center for Devices and Radiological Health. Available online at <http://www.fda.gov/cdrh/devadvice/314.html>.

Rubin, Avi, Tadayoshi Kohno, Adam Stubblefield, and Dan S. Wallach. 2004. "Analysis of an Electronic Voting System." *IEEE Symposium on Security and Privacy*, Oakland, Calif. Available online at <http://avirubin.com/vote.pdf>.

Sarter, N., and D.D. Woods. 1995. "How in the World Did We Get into That Mode? Mode Error and Awareness in Supervisory Control." *Human Factors* 37:5-19.

Sarter, N., D.D. Woods, and C. Billings. 1997. "Automation Surprises," *Handbook of Human Factors/Ergonomics*, G. Salvendy, ed., 2nd Ed., Wiley, New York, pp. 1926-1943. (Reprinted in N. Moray, ed., *Ergonomics: Major Writings*, Taylor & Francis, Boca Raton, Fla., 2004.)

Schneider, Fred. 2000. "Enforceable Security Policies." *ACM Transactions on Information and System Security (TISSEC)* 3(1):30-50.

Sha, Lui. 2001. "Using Simplicity to Control Complexity." *IEEE Software* 18(4):20-28.

Shankland, Stephen. 2003. "SuSE Linux gets security credentials." *CNET News.com*, August 5. Available online at <http://news.com.com/2100-1016_3-5059846.html?tag=fd_top>.

Shooman, M.L. 1996. "Avionics Software Problem Occurrence Rates." *The Seventh International Symposium on Software Reliability Engineering* (ISSRE '96), p. 55. Available online at <http://doi.ieeecomputersociety.org/10.1109/ISSRE.1996.558695>.

Shortliffe, Edward H. 2005. "Strategic Action in Health Information Technology: Why the Obvious Has Taken So Long." *Health Affairs* 24(5):1222-1233.

Slabodkin, Gregory. 1998. "Software Glitches Leave Navy Smart Ship Dead in the Water." *Government Computer News*, July 13. Available online at <http://www.gcn.com/print/17_17/33727-1.html>.

Smith, P.J., E. McCoy, and C. Layton. 1997. "Brittleness in the Design of Cooperative Problem-Solving Systems: The Effects on User Performance." *IEEE Transactions on Systems, Man and Cybernetics—Part A* 27(3):360-371.

Starbuck, W.H., and M. Farjoun, eds. 2005. *Organization at the Limit: NASA and the Columbia Disaster*. Blackwell, Malden, Mass.

"Tanker Truck Shutdown via Satellite." 2004. *GPS News*, November 4. Available online at <http://www.spacedaily.com/news/gps-03zn.html>.

Taylor, Andrew. 2001. "IT Projects Sink or Swim," Based on author's M.B.A. dissertation, *BCS Review*.

Thibodeau, Patrick. 2003. "NASA Leads Efforts to Build Better Software." *Computerworld*, February 7. Available online at <http://www.computerworld.com/softwaretopics/software/story/0,10801,78362,00.html>.

Tiernan, Ray. 2003. "When Computing Was Reliable." *osOpinion.com*, March 17.

Trimble, Stephen. 2005. "Avionics Redesign Aims to Improve F/A-22 Stability." *Flight International*, August 23.

Verton, Dan. 2003. "GAO Reports Focused on NASA IT Workforce Issues." *Computerworld*, February 4. Available online at <http://www.computerworld.com/careertopics/careers/labor/story/0,10801,78172,00.html>.

Wall, Robert. 2003. "Code Red Emergency." *Aviation Week & Space Technology*, June 9, pp. 35-36.

Wears, Robert L., and Marc Berg. 2005. "Computer Technology and Clinical Work: Still Waiting for Godot." *Journal of the American Medical Association* 293:1261-1263.

Weaver, Nicholas, and Vern Paxson. 2004. "A Worst-Case Worm." Paper presented at the Third Annual Workshop on Economics and Information Security (WEIS04), March 13-14. Available online at <http://www.dtc.umn.edu/weis2004/weaver.pdf>.

Williams, Laurie, Robert R. Kessler, Ward Cunningham, and Ron Jeffries. 2000. "Strengthening the Case for Pair Programming." *IEEE Software* 17(4):19-25.

Woods, D.D., and E. Hollnagel. 2006. *Joint Cognitive Systems: Patterns in Cognitive Systems Engineering*. Taylor & Francis, Boca Raton, Fla.

Yurcik, William, and David Doss. 2001. "Achieving Fault-Tolerant Software with Rejuvenation and Reconfiguration." *IEEE Software* 18(4):48-52.

Yurcik, William, and David Doss. 2002. "Software Technology Issues for a U.S. National Missile Defense System." *IEEE Technology and Society Magazine* 21(2):36-46.

Appendixes

A

Biographies of Committee Members and Staff

COMMITTEE MEMBERS

Daniel Jackson (*Chair*) is a professor of computer science at the Massachusetts Institute of Technology (MIT). He received an M.A. from Oxford University (1984) in physics and an S.M. (1988) and Ph.D. (1992) from MIT in computer science. He was a software engineer for Logica UK Ltd. (1984-1986) and an assistant professor of computer science at Carnegie Mellon University (1992-1997). He has broad interests in many areas of software engineering, especially in specification and design, critical systems, formal methods, static analysis, and model checking. Dr. Jackson is the author of *Software Abstractions: Logic, Language, and Analysis* (MIT Press, 2006).

Joshua Bloch is a principal software engineer at Google. Previously he was a distinguished engineer at Sun Microsystems, where he was an architect in the Core Java Platform Group. He wrote the bestselling book *Effective Java*, winner of the 2002 Jolt Award. He led the design and implementation of many parts of the Java platform, including the collections framework, Tiger language enhancements (JSR-201), annotations (JSR-175), multiprecision arithmetic, preferences (JSR-10), and assertions (JSR-41). Previously he was a senior systems designer at Transarc Corporation, where he designed and implemented many parts of the Encina distributed transaction processing system. He holds a Ph.D. in computer science from Carnegie Mellon University and a B.S. in computer science from Columbia University.

Michael DeWalt is chief scientist, aviation systems, for Certification Services, Inc., a Seattle-area aviation consultancy. Mr. DeWalt is authorized by the FAA, as a consultant designated engineering representative (DER), to approve software for any aircraft system, at any software level. In addition to his DER duties, he helps clients who have unusual project requirements to develop acceptable software-approval techniques. For 11 years, he was the FAA's national resource specialist for aircraft software. He was responsible for starting the international committee that created DO-178B and served as its secretary. He was also secretary of the committee that created DO-248B and DO-278. Mr. DeWalt has been involved with both civil and military software avionics and certification for 26 years, working for airframe manufacturers and avionics suppliers. In addition to his DER certificate, he has a B.S.E.E., a master's in software engineering, and a commercial pilot's license.

Reed Gardner is a professor and chair of the Department of Medical Informatics at the University of Utah. He has been a codirector of medical computing at LDS, Cottonwood, and Alta View Hospitals in Salt Lake City. He is one of the principal developers and evaluators of the medical expert system known as HELP (Health Evaluation through Logical Processing). Dr. Gardner's primary academic and research interests are evaluating the benefits of medical expert systems as they relate to quality and cost-effectiveness; development of software oversight committee methods for evaluation of safety and effectiveness of medical software and systems; public health informatics; applying computers in intensive-care medicine; and developing devices and communications methods to acquire patient data at the bedside. He is the author or coauthor of more than 300 articles in the fields of medical informatics and engineering. Dr. Gardner has been a journal editor and on the editorial boards of *Critical Care Medicine* and other critical care journals as well as the *Journal of the American Medical Informatics Association* (JAMIA). He is a fellow of the American College of Medical Informatics and past president of the American Medical Informatics Association. Dr. Gardner holds a B.S.E.E. from the University of Utah (1960) in electrical engineering and a Ph.D. from the University of Utah (1968) in biophysics and bioengineering.

Peter Lee is a professor of computer science at Carnegie Mellon University. He joined the faculty of Carnegie Mellon's School of Computer Science in 1987, after completing his doctoral studies at the University of Michigan. He is known internationally for his research contributions in areas related to information assurance, especially the application of programming language technology to operating systems design, networking, and computer security. Dr. Lee is best known for his co-invention of the proof-carrying code technology for ensuring the security of mobile code. Today, proof-carrying code is the subject of several DARPA- and NSF-sponsored research projects and forms the basis for the products and services provided by Cedilla Systems Incorporated, a Java technology start-up company he cofounded in 1999. Dr. Lee is also the associate dean for undergraduate education in Carnegie Mellon's School of Computer Science. In this capacity, he has been involved in the administration of Carnegie Mellon's undergraduate programs in computer science. His tenure as associate dean has seen the undergraduate program rise to national prominence, both for its intensive problem-oriented curriculum and for its success in attracting and retaining women in the field of computer science. He has published extensively in major international symposia and is the author of two books. He has been invited to give distinguished lectures and keynote addresses at major universities and symposia and has been called on as an expert witness in key judicial court cases such as the *Sun v. Microsoft* "Java lawsuit." Dr. Lee has also been a member of the Army Science Board since 1997, for which he has served on four major summer studies, and the co-chair of a technology panel for the 2001 Defense Science Board study on defense science and technology. In addition to holding M.S. and Ph.D. degrees in computer and communication sciences, Dr. Lee earned a B.S. in mathematics from the University of Michigan in 1982. He has been a principal investigator on several DARPA, NSF, and NASA grants and contracts.

Steven B. Lipner is senior director of security engineering strategy at Microsoft. He is responsible for defining Microsoft's Security Development Lifecycle and the plans for its evolution and application to new product generations. His team also defines and executes programs to help Microsoft customers deploy and operate their systems securely. Mr. Lipner has been at Microsoft since 1999. He joined the company after working at Trusted Information Systems, the MITRE Corporation, and Digital Equipment Corporation, among others. He has more than 35 years' experience in computer and network security as a researcher, development manager, and business unit manager. He holds 11 patents in computer and network security and served two terms as a member of the U.S. Information Security and Privacy Advisory Board. Mr. Lipner is coauthor with Michael Howard of *The Security Development Lifecycle*. He holds an M.S. (1966) in civil engineering from MIT and attended the Program for Management Development at the Harvard Graduate School of Business Administration.

Charles Perrow is a professor emeritus of sociology at Yale University. He was a vice president of the Eastern Sociological Society; a fellow of the Center for Advanced Study in the Behavioral Sciences; fellow of the American Academy for the Advancement of Science; resident scholar at the Russell Sage Foundation; fellow, Shelly Cullom Davis Center for Historical Studies; visitor, Institute for Advanced Study; and a former member of the National Research Council's Committee on Human Factors, the Sociology Panel of the National Science Foundation, and of the editorial boards of several journals. An organizational theorist, he is the author of six books—*The Radical Attack on Business*; *Organizational Analysis: A Sociological View*; *Complex Organizations: A Critical Essay*; *Normal Accidents: Living with High Risk Technologies*; *The AIDS Disaster: The Failure of Organizations in New York and the Nation*, with Mauro Guillen; *Organizing America: Wealth, Power, and the Origins of American Capitalism*—and over 50 articles. His current interests are in managing complexly interactive, tightly coupled systems (including hospitals, nuclear plants, power grids, the space program, and intelligent transportation systems); the challenge and limits of network-centric warfare; self-organizing properties of the Internet, the electric power grid, networks of small firms, and terrorist organizations; and the possibilities for restructuring society to reduce our increasing vulnerability to disasters, whether natural, industrial/technological, or deliberate. These interests grow out of his work on "normal accidents," with its emphasis on organizational design and systems theory, and reflect current consultations and workshops with NASA, the FAA, Naval War College, DaimlerChrysler, NIH, and NSF.

Jon Pincus is the general manager of strategy development in Microsoft's Online Services Group, where he leads a broad-based effort to develop, analyze, work for the adoption of, and execute game-changing strategies in the online services space. Key principles include a global focus, user-centricity, attention to perspectives other than the usual ones, virtuous-cycle ecosystems, and leveraging Microsoft's assets. In his previous role in the Systems and Networking Group at Microsoft Research, he focused on security, privacy, and reliability of software and software-based systems. His major interests include applying perspectives and insights from the social sciences and humanities to the construction and application of these systems (which inevitably blends into cultural issues throughout the disciplines of software engineering and computer science, as well as at Microsoft and other organizations that produce software and systems); measurement of security and privacy; and the exploitation and mitigation of low-level programming defects such as buffer overruns. In his pre-Microsoft days, he was founder and chief technology officer at Intrinsa, which was acquired by Microsoft in 1999 along with PREfix and the rest of the company's assets. He has also worked in design automation (placement and routing for ICs and CAD frameworks) at GE Calma and EDA Systems.

John Rushby is program director for formal methods and dependable systems at SRI International. He worked at the Atlas Computer Laboratory (now part of the Computation and Information Department of the Central Laboratory of the U.K. Research Councils), as a lecturer in the Computer Science Department at Manchester University, and as a research associate in the Department of Computing Science at the University of Newcastle upon Tyne, before joining SRI in 1983. At SRI, he was successively promoted to computer scientist, senior computer scientist, program manager and, from 1986 to 1990, the acting director of CSL. In 1991 Dr. Rushby assumed his current role as program director. He is interested primarily in the design and assurance of critical systems, including properties such as security and safety, mechanisms such as kernelization and fault tolerance, and formal methods for assurance. He considers the main value of formal methods to lie in their use for constructing mathematical models whose properties can be analyzed and verified by computational means. This has led him to focus on the development of effective tools for formal methods. Dr. Rushby holds a Ph.D. in computer science from the University of Newcastle (1977).

Lui Sha holds a Ph.D. and an M.S. in electrical and computer engineering from Carnegie Mellon University and a B.S.E.E. from McGill University. He is Donald B. Gillies Chair professor of computer science at the University of Illinois at Urbana-Champaign. Before joining UIUC in 1998, he was a senior member of the technical staff at the Software Engineering Institute at Carnegie Mellon University, which he joined in 1986. He is a fellow of the ACM and a fellow of the IEEE for "technical leadership and research contributions which enabled the transformation of real-time computing practice from an ad hoc process to an engineering process based on analytic methods." He was the chair of the IEEE Real-Time Systems Technical Committee from 1999 to 2000 and received that committee's Outstanding Technical Contributions and Leadership Award in December 2001. Dr. Sha's accomplishments are many. He led the development of Generalized Rate Monotonic theory, which has transformed hardware and software open standards in real-time computing; has been supported by nearly all the commercially available real-time operating systems, middleware, and modeling tools; and has been taught in real-time computing courses around the world. His work was cited in the selected accomplishment section of the 1992 National Academy of Science's report *Computing the Future: A Broader Agenda for Computer Science and Engineering.* His expertise in dependable real-time computing systems has made him an indispensable resource for many national high-technology projects, including critical assistance to the International Space Station, the Global Positioning System software upgrade, Mars Pathfinder, F-22 avionics stability improvement, and F35 mission system architecture.

Martyn Thomas graduated as a biochemist from University College, London, and immediately entered the computer industry. From 1969 to 1983, he worked in universities (in London and the Netherlands), in industry (designing switching software for STC), and at the South West Universities Regional Computer Centre in Bath. In 1983 (with David Bean), he founded a software engineering company, Praxis, to exploit modern software development methods. In December 1992, Praxis was sold to Deloitte and Touche, an international firm of accountants and management consultants, and Mr. Thomas became a Deloitte Consulting international partner while remaining chair and, later, managing director of Praxis. He left Deloitte Consulting in 1997. Mr. Thomas is now an independent consultant software engineer specializing in the assessment of large, real-time, safety-critical, software-intensive systems, software engineering, and engineering management. He serves as an expert witness where complex software engineering issues are involved. He is a visiting professor in software engineering at the University of Oxford and a visiting professor at the University of Bristol and the University of Wales, Aberystwyth. He has advised the U.K. government and the Commission of the European Union on policy in the fields of software engineering and VLSI design. He has had close links with the academic research community throughout his career, as a member of two University Funding Council research assessments in computer science, numerous international conference program committees, and several U.K. government and Research Council panels and boards. He has been a member of the IT Foresight Panel of the U.K. Government Office of Science and Technology, a member of the advisory board for the DERA Systems and Software Engineering Centre, and a member of the Research Advisory Council of the U.K. Civil Aviation Authority. He is a fellow of the British Computer Society and of the Institution of Engineering and Technology. He currently serves on the Engineering and Technology Strategic Panel of the British Computer Society, the IT sector panel of the IET, the advisory group to the Foresight Cyber Trust and Crime Prevention Project, the executive of the U.K. Computing Research Committee, and as a member of the advisory council of the Foundation for Information Policy Research. He is chair of the steering committee for the U.K. Interdisciplinary Research Collaboration on Dependable Systems (DIRC) and a former member of the the U.K. Engineering and Physical Sciences Research Council. In 2007, he was awarded the Commander of the Order of the British Empire (CBE) for services to software engineering.

Scott Wallsten is a senior fellow and director of communications policy studies at the Progress and Freedom Foundation (PFF) and also a lecturer in Stanford University's public policy program. Before joining PFF he was a senior fellow at the American Enterprise Institute (AEI)-Brookings Joint Center for Regulatory Studies and a resident scholar at the AEI. He has also served as an economist at The World Bank, a scholar at the Stanford Institute for Economic Policy Research, and a staff economist at the U.S. President's Council of Economic Advisers. Dr. Wallsten's interests include industrial organization and public policy, and his research has focused on regulation, privatization, competition, and science and technology policy. His work has been published in numerous academic journals, including the *RAND Journal of Economics*, the *Journal of Industrial Economics*, the *Journal of Regulatory Economics*, and *Regulation*, and his commentaries have appeared in newspapers throughout the world. He has a Ph.D. in economics from Stanford University.

David Woods is a professor in the Institute for Ergonomics at the Ohio State University. He was president (1998-1999) and is a fellow of the Human Factors and Ergonomic Society and is also a fellow of the American Psychological Society and the American Psychological Association. He has received the Ely Award for best paper in the journal *Human Factors*, the Kraft Innovators Award from the Human Factors and Ergonomic Society for developing the foundations of cognitive engineering, a Laurels Award from *Aviation Week and Space Technology* for research on the human factors of highly automated cockpits, an IBM Faculty Award, and five patents for computerized decision aids. He was on the board of the National Patient Safety Foundation from its founding until 2002 and was associate director of the Midwest Center for Inquiry on Patient Safety (GAPS Center) of the Veterans Health Administration from 1999 to 2003. He is coauthor of the monographs *Behind Human Error* and *A Tale of Two Stories: Contrasting Views of Patient Safety* and the books *Joint Cognitive Systems: Foundations of Cognitive Systems Engineering* and *Joint Cognitive Systems: Patterns in Cognitive Systems Engineering*, and co-editor of *Resilience Engineering*. His research includes studies of data overload in control centers, critical care medicine, and inferential analysis; field studies of team work between people; and automation in anesthesiology, aviation, space mission operations, disaster response, and health care. His work on how to make systems resilient to improve safety is based on accident investigations in nuclear power, medicine, and space operations. Multimedia overviews of his research are available at <http://csel.eng.

ohio-state.edu/woods/>. Based on this body of work, he has been an advisor to various government agencies and other organizations on issues pertaining to human performance and error, including the Federal Aviation Administration, Nuclear Regulatory Commission, National Patient Safety Foundation, Veterans Health Administration, and National Science Foundation, and was an advisor to the Columbia Accident Investigation Board. Most recently he served on a National Academy of Engineering/ Institute of Medicine study panel that applied engineering to improve health care systems and on a National Research Council panel that defined the future of the national air transportation system. Dr. Woods earned a Ph.D. from Purdue University in 1979.

STAFF

Lynette I. Millett is a senior program officer and study director at the Computer Science and Telecommunications Board of the National Academies. She is currently involved in several CSTB projects, including a study on software-intensive systems producibility, an assessment of the Social Security Administration's e-government strategy, and a comprehensive exploration of biometrics systems, among other things. She was the study director for the CSTB project that produced *Who Goes There? Authentication Technologies and Their Privacy Implications* and *IDs—Not That Easy: Questions About Nationwide Identity Systems*. Her portfolio includes significant portions of CSTB's recent work on software and on identity systems and privacy. She has an M.Sc. in computer science from Cornell University, along with a B.A. in mathematics and computer science with honors from Colby College. Her graduate work was supported by both an NSF graduate fellowship and an Intel graduate fellowship.

David Padgham rejoined CSTB as an associate program officer in the spring of 2006 following nearly 2 years as a policy analyst in the Association for Computing Machinery's (ACM's) Washington, D.C., Office of Public Policy, where he worked closely with that organization's public policy committee, USACM. Previously, Mr. Padgham spent nearly 6 years with CSTB, working on—among other things—the studies that produced *Trust in Cyberspace; Funding a Revolution; Broadband: Bringing Home the Bits; LC21: A Digital Strategy for the Library of Congress;* and *The Internet's Coming of Age*. Currently, he is focused on the CSTB projects related to health care informatics, computing performance, and software dependability. He holds a master's degree in library and information science from the Catholic University of America in Washington, D.C., and a bachelor of arts degree in English from Warren Wilson College in Asheville, N.C.

Gloria Westbrook recently left the Computer Science and Telecommunications Board where she was a senior program assistant. She previously served as the executive assistant to the directors of the Office of Youth Programs and the Youth Opportunity Grant Program at the D.C. Department of Employment Services (DOES). In 2003, Ms. Westbrook was selected to be the lead administrator of a team that successfully administered a $4 million Summer Youth Employment Program that registered over 5,000 District youth. In addition, Ms. Westbrook has also served as the executive assistant to the director of DOES, where she was appointed by the director to serve as his elite liaison to the D.C. mayor and his cabinet, members of the D.C. Council, and members of Congress. While serving in the Director's Office, Ms. Westbrook received the Meritorious Service Award and the Workforce Development Administrator's Award of Appreciation for Dedication of Service. She also became a member of the National Association of Executive Secretaries and Administrative Assistants. She attended Duke Ellington School of the Performing Arts for ballet and went on to further her dance education at the University of the Arts in Philadelphia.

Phil Hilliard was a research associate with the Computer Science and Telecommunications Board until May 2004. He provided research support as part of the professional staff and worked on projects focusing on telecommunications research, supercomputing, and dependable systems. Before joining the National Academies, he worked at BellSouth in Atlanta, Georgia, as a competitive intelligence analyst and at NCR as a technical writer and trainer. He has a master's in library and information science from Florida State University, an M.B.A. from Georgia State University, and a B.S. in computer and information technology from the Georgia Institute of Technology.

Penelope Smith worked temporarily with the Computer Science and Telecommunications Board between February and July 2004 as a senior program assistant. Prior to joining the National Academies, she worked in rural Angola as a health project manager and community health advisor for Concern Worldwide. She also worked for Emory University as a project coordinator and researcher on reproductive health and HIV and for the Centers for Disease Control as a technology transfer evaluator for HIV/AIDS programs. She earned an M.P.H. from Emory University and a B.A. in medical anthropology from the University of California at Santa Cruz. She is also a certified health education specialist.

B

Open Session Briefers

Although the individuals listed below provided much useful information of various kinds to the committee, they were not asked to endorse this study's conclusions or recommendations, nor did they see the final draft of this report before its release.

DECEMBER 18-19, 2003
WASHINGTON, D.C.

Helen Gill, National Science Foundation
Sol Greenspan, National Science Foundation
Paul L. Jones, Food and Drug Administration
Carl Landwehr, National Science Foundation
Ernie Lucier, Federal Aviation Administration
Brad Martin, National Security Agency
Paul Miner, NASA
Ralph Wachter, Office of Naval Research

APRIL 19-21, 2004
WORKSHOP ON SOFTWARE
CERTIFICATION AND DEPENDABILITY
WASHINGTON, D.C.

Kent Beck, Three Rivers Institute
Richard Cook, University of Chicago

David Dill, Stanford University
Matthias Felleisen, Northeastern University
Brent Goldfarb, University of Maryland
Anthony Hall, Praxis Critical Systems
Bob Harper, Carnegie Mellon University
Mats Heimdahl, University of Minnesota
Chuck Howell, MITRE Corporation
Doug Jones, University of Iowa
Shriram Krishnamurthi, Brown University
Jim Larus, Microsoft Research
Isaac Levendel, Independent Consultant
Gary McGraw, Cigital
Peter Neumann, SRI International
Bob Noel, MITRE Corporation
Gene Rochlin, University of California, Berkeley
Avi Rubin, Johns Hopkins University
Bill Scherlis, Carnegie Mellon University
Ted Selker, Massachusetts Institute of Technology
André van Tilborg, Office of the Secretary of Defense

MAY 18-19, 2004
CAMBRIDGE, MASSACHUSETTS

James Baker, U.S. Air Force
Michael Cusumano, Massachusetts Institute of Technology
Michael Hammer, Hammer and Company
Mike Lai, Microsoft
Butler Lampson, Microsoft Research
Alfred Spector, IBM Research
Richard Stanley, MITRE

FEBRUARY 16-18, 2005
MOUNTAIN VIEW, CALIFORNIA

Bill Bush, Sun Microsystems
Window Snyder, Microsoft

C

Statement of Task

This project will convene a mixed group of experts to assess current practices for developing and evaluating mission-critical software, with an emphasis on dependability objectives. The goal of this study is to identify the kinds of system properties for which certification is desired, how that certification is obtained today, and, most important, what design and development methods, including methods for establishing evidence of trustworthiness, could lead to future systems structures that are more easily certified. Where these methods cannot be identified, the study will identify a research agenda that would lead to their discovery. The committee will address system certification, examining a few different application domains (e.g., medical devices and aviation systems) and their approaches to software evaluation and assurance. This should provide some understanding of what common ground and disparities exist.

The discussion will engage members of the fundamental research community, who have been scarce in this arena. It will consider approaches to systematically assessing systems' user interfaces. It will examine potential benefits and costs of improvements in evaluation of dependability as performance dimensions. It will evaluate the extent to which current tools and techniques aid in ensuring and evaluating dependability in software and investigate technology that might support changes in the development and certification process. It will also use the information amassed to develop a research agenda for dependable software system development and certification, factoring in earlier High Confidence Software and

Systems research planning. It will also investigate ideas for improving the certification processes for dependability-critical software systems. The work of the expert committee will culminate in a written report with recommendations, which will be subject to National Research Council review processes.